NUMINOUS ANIMAL

WRITING IN RESIDENCE

ISSN 2818-730X (Print) ISSN 2818-7318 (Online)

The Writing in Residence series brings together a diverse range of texts by the artists invited to Athabasca University's Writer in Residence program. Each volume showcases the exceptional talents of these established writers, resulting in works presented in a variety of genres, from essays and personal reflections to memoir, poetry, and conversational interviews. These innovative works provide an opportunity to celebrate contributions made by prominent literary figures and highlight Athabasca University's commitment to fostering literary excellence.

SERIES TITLES

The Virtues of Disillusionment • Steven Heighton • *Indigiqueerness: A Conversation about Storytelling* • Joshua Whitehead, in dialogue with Angie Abdou • *Writing Ukraine* • Myrna Kostash • *My Works, Ye Mighty* • Christian Bök • *Numinous Animal: Tracing the Afro-futurism of Black Cowboys* • Bertrand Bickersteth

TRACING THE AFROFUTURISM OF BLACK COWBOYS

NUMINOUS ANIMAL

BERTRAND BICKERSTETH

AU PRESS

CONTENTS

FOREWORD

What is this book? That should be an easy question to answer, but Bertrand Bickersteth has the unwieldly mind of a poet, and, in *Numinous Animal*, he lets readers into that kaleidoscope world. He reveals history where we've only known blanks. He argues for unity where authorities have consistently portrayed contradictions. He finds fractures and fragments in narratives previously perceived as linear, whole, and uncomplicated. By Bickersteth's own admission, he has written an "odd" book, and he wonders how its wide-ranging ideas come together or if they should even come together at all.

To summarize the project most simply (too simply!), Bertrand Bickersteth has created an original typeface formed from cattle brands of Black cowboys, and *Numinous Animal* explains why he did so and what he hopes to achieve with this esoteric alphabet. Bickersteth claims that the creation of his new font is a political act of reclamation. In explaining the project, Bickersteth shares his own personal history, the history of Black cowboys, particularly in Alberta, and some of the history of Sierra Leone, where he was born and from where he moved to Canada as an infant.

In short, then, *Numinous Animal* provides a history of Bertrand Bickersteth, as well as a rational and political context for Bertrand Bickersteth's font.

But the book does more. To attempt to summarize this text is to diminish it. *Numinous Animal* is a poet's creation – complex, non-linear, fluid, unexpected, full of juxtapositions and original leaps. Is it a history? A theoretical treatise on race? A decolonization project? A poem? A memoir? An instruction booklet? An introduction of a new font? A genealogy? A reflection on the role of poetry? A rebellion against historical and ongoing stories of erasure? A linguistic analysis? A research report on immigration history and its effects? An act of theft (wherein Bickersteth finds a history stolen from him and steals it back)? Is the book a gift? A reclamation? A promise?

Yes. *Numinous Animal* is a bit of all of that. The narrative is sprawling and unrestrained, as are its ideas. Sometimes Bickersteth looks backwards to untold, forgotten histories, and other times he reaches forwards to a promise for tomorrow. Sometimes his style is academic and formal, other times relaxed and colloquial, and, at yet other points, poetic. Sometimes the author shows up on the page rigorously interrogative. Other times he comes across as playful or self-deprecating or nostalgic. Sometimes he tells stories. Sometimes he dismantles stereotypes. Sometimes he shares strategies (for recovering lost histories, for understanding identity and hybridity, for survival).

Each time I come back to the pages of *Numinous Animal*, I find a different kind of text, a different way of knowing, a fresh understanding. I try to hold the book up to the light, get a good grasp on it, know it for what it really is – but full control slides away. Each attempt is a kind of failure in that I always fall short, again, of being able to claim full understanding, to clearly name it. But each attempt is also a success because with each reading, I see new aspects, another throughline, a fresh insight to explore, an original idea to play with. This slippery, sometimes ineffable, quality of *Numinous Animal*, its resistance to easy labels, is perfect, given the insistence with which it calls into question the very act of naming. Leave it to a poet to make certain that the structure and style mirror the content.

In his reflection on hybridity and identity, Bickersteth poses many interesting questions specifically relevant to himself and his own experiences, like how can a Black writer appropriate Black history? He explores whose histories he can claim and whose stories apply to him, helping to build his own story as an African in Alberta and an Albertan out of Africa. He also poses questions more wider reaching, questions which might apply to any reader's experience, like how do we relate to home when home feels inhospitable? Or how does one create a coherent identity out of a fractured and sometimes opaque past? That's one thing that becomes very clear in these pages: Bickersteth quite likes questions. He never passively accepts any (hi)stories. He always investigates, questions, disrupts.

In fact, we might say that the alphabet-by-cattle-brand project has its genesis in a series of Bickersteth's questions – what if I created my own typeface? How would I do so in a way to capture this lost history (an erasure that has caused us to forget that one in four cowboys was Black)? Is it even possible to create a font out of cattle brands? What is the connection between cattle brands and fashion brands? How does the physical reality of branding as scarring connect, literally and metaphorically, to the history – and erasure – of Black cowboys?

And so on.

Bickersteth's questions are infinite.

This interrogative spirit is central to *Numinous Animal* and to Bickersteth's larger project. I suspect that the same energetic, insatiable curiosity is a key quality of Bickersteth himself. *Numinous Animal* is the product of that beautiful curiosity. My hope is that readers meet the book with the same deep, playful, dynamic curiosity. Doing so will be rewarded and rewarded again, as the pages offer up new gifts with each new engagement.

ANGIE ABDOU
Writer in Residence Program Committee,
Faculty of Humanities and Social Sciences, Athabasca University

INTRODUCTION

Numinous Animal is an odd book. When I first started it, I wasn't sure what I was writing. I resolved to keep going and allow its shape to reveal itself eventually. But 10,000 words into the project, it only felt like a weird hybrid – somewhere between biography, a regional history, and a classroom slide presentation. Nothing was coming together. What's more, there was a nagging question of *should* those three things be coming together at all? It took some work to get there, but now I see the hybridity of this book as its central feature – its dimensionality a necessary structure. At one point during the writing, it occurred to me that one of my biggest influences – James Baldwin – had already written a similar kind of hybrid. *No Name on the Street* is sometimes considered social memoir because it never cleanly separates itself from one or the other genre. I should be so lucky as to consider myself in the same general category as James Baldwin, but I do think we both, at least, share the concern for how one relates to "home" when home feels inhospitable at best, hostile at worst. We certainly share an anger at being forced into having to contend with these two constricting sides of home. In fact, for many years of my life, anger was my go-to tool for coping with this insufferable situation. As it turns out, it is necessary to grapple with the history that one has inherited in order to properly come to grips with one's anger, with the hows and whys of home's inhospitality. Anger has its problems, Baldwin shows me, and at the same time he reminds me that anger also has its uses.

Only after I finished this manuscript did it occur to me that it also has a modern template in Saidiya Hartman's *Lose Your Mother*, a text that effortlessly straddles the personal and the historical. I might have felt more confident sooner in the writing process had I thought of these works, but as it was, I discovered my own legitimizing pathway forward and settled into its groove. The pathway was literally another form of waymaking: trails, specifically cowboy trails. These meandering paths are historic but they are also deeply personal. They follow very specific directions, linking ranches to markets, but they also follow natural contours of the land. Herding cannot move as the crow flies, from point A to point B. It must adapt to the landscape; it must allow for watering and grazing, which, again, is dictated by where and what the land offers up. And in this sense, it is once more deeply historical: trails do not spring up instantly out of the demands that markets make, but they have been shaped by traditions that have been listening to the language of the landscape for millennia. Cowboys followed trails already long established by Indigenous peoples; Indigenous communities followed trails created by the wildlife they were in rhythm with; the wildlife pursued patterns of vegetation that inspired the rhythm. I offer up this book in that tradition of purposeful, meandering music. It moves from idea to idea, from biography to history, from North America to Africa. It moves purposefully, slowly, around bends, along contours. It meanders musically.

In an important way, anger is also a part of that meandering music. Here's how: I once received an email that really took me aback. It began, more or less, with the words "how dare you," and carried on from there, spitting venom and fury for five or six paragraphs. The cause for this anger was an article I had written: an encyclopedia entry for Black fur traders. If you find that surprising, so did I. Encyclopedic entries are not the usual category to drum up outrage from a reader. What surprised me even more, though, is that my detractor was Black, or to be accurate, Afro-Indigenous. Most of my writing is dedicated to restoring the lost, ignored, or dismissed histories of Black communities in this part of the world. I've only ever received encouragement or gratitude or solidarity from people of African and/or Indigenous descent who have read my work. Receiving an angry message from someone who is usually allied with me was disorienting, to say the least. I would like to think that my writing about history is dynamic enough to deserve the heightened emotions of this email, but mulling over portage trails and detailing the canoeing duties of middlemen hardly merited the reaction it got in this case. From what I could tell, though, in the plaintiff's mind there was actually nothing wrong with the content of what I had written. The problem was that I had written it at all. In other words, the problem was representation and appropriation. This actually made me pause.

It is not an accusation I have ever faced before in any sense, but even less did I expect to encounter it with respect to my writing about Black history. How could I, a Black writer, appropriate Black history in my work? As far-fetched as it might have seemed, some instinct in me wasn't ready to dismiss the complaint as ill-conceived and just drop the question as irrelevant. While I didn't agree with the thrust of the argument that was made in the email, it did open up a line of questioning that never would have occurred to me otherwise. What right do I have to represent histories that I do not directly access through lineage or community participation? Of course, I am rigorous in my historical explorations, and I can always retort that no one else was writing these histories and so — appropriation or not — I am responsible for showing them the light of day. But as a question, it is valid, and I've considered it repeatedly in all of my writing ever since. In fact, this book, *Numinous Animal*, is very much a furthering of that question directly applied to the Albertan context. Most of my writing is concerned with Black history on the Prairies, and I take the responsibility of engaging that topic personally. However, I have no personal or family history rooted in this region. My family immigrated to Canada from West Africa. So what claims can I make on Black Alberta's historical roots? That is the question at the heart of this book.

It began with my tenure as writer in residence at Athabasca University throughout 2024–25. The major project I worked on in that role was a collection of poems based on the lives of Black cowboys and ranchers at the end of the nineteenth and beginning of the twentieth centuries. The joy of that project was in representing the lives of these forgotten figures, along with researching and discovering any cattle brands they may have registered at the time. To my pleasure, I found about a dozen. The culmination of that project is this book's turn to Afrofuturism: a font I developed based on the designs of the cattle brands I had found. Identifying the marks of Black historical figures who had been forgotten felt like an important recovery. But it inspired me to go further. Discussing them in a book is thrilling, of course, but let's face it, books only have limited scope, limited impact. I wanted to return this lost history to our present times in a central, fundamental way. Afrofuturism is ambitious. It is not just fixed on the future, but accommodates dualities, particularly the incorporation of the past – of history – in the living possibilities for what might come. The idea of creating a font fit this ambition perfectly. On the one hand, I could compose some of the poetry using this font; in this way, the object of the poetry becomes the subject – the poetry is not just about Black cowboys but is also composed in collaboration with their designing minds, their expressions of individuality, their poetic impulses. On the other hand, I could make the font available to the public, so that these designs become a general part of everyday life in random documents, emails, texting. Both aspects – the precise poetry and the random texts – represent powerful acts of reclamation that I felt others would find important as well, not just me.

Numinous Animal charts the process of developing this font. But it is much more than that. Because the development of the font demanded the recovery of certain historical narratives, this book also had to be about the recovery of those narratives. And because my angry emailer remains on my mind with any historical project I consider, I had to reckon with the appropriateness of making any kinds of claims on the histories of Black cowboys in this region. To me, this one felt easier to accomplish because I'm from this region and I grew up immersed in particular icons of "Albertaness" which included cowboys (and homesteaders and oil rigs, etc.). Yet, I didn't want to take that for granted. If anything, my angry emailer reminded me of the care that every historian should take with their subject (topic) and their subjectivity (agency). And so *Numinous Animal* became as much a confrontation with my personal claims on Black history from this part of the world as it was a revelation of that history and how it impacted my poetic practice. Spoiler alert: I win the confrontation. But that's because this thing called Blackness, which was not enough to appease my angry emailer, is a flattening thing that forces people into relation, who under almost any other circumstance – noted by my angry emailer's anger – would have no relation to each other. But in this sense, I also lose the confrontation. We all do. Because we didn't choose that flattening. I didn't choose to be forced into a relation with my angry emailer. But I am. As he is with me. History forced us together and therefore I am forced to make claims on the many tangled threads of that history. As carefully, and, yes, as angrily as I can.

Calgary, 30 December 2025

PART 1

PARTY ANIMALS

THE PARTY

Somewhere around eleven o'clock in the evening, the party my parents were throwing for one of my aunts hit its euphoric high: King Sunny Ade boomed out; the Africans pounced onto the dance floor like Olympic athletes, everyone chasing a medal, everyone confident in their ability to win a medal, everyone glorying in the rhythm of summer that pulsed through these Games.

I know it is a stereotype to describe Africans dancing in joy, but I truly grew up with this particular stereotype. There might be a tendency for white North Americans not to take Africans seriously; that is, there might be a tendency for them to see Africans as either harmless and happy, or self-harming and tragic. The truth is, dance is just one of the many aspects of their human dimensionality. They inherited it like we in Canada inherit an understanding of hockey's importance. We may not play it. We may not even like it. But we understand the centrality it holds, and we can access that understanding at the drop of a hat. As it was, my parents and the unique Prairie African community they belonged to – indeed, that they helped to shape – had that same instantaneous access to dance. North Americans are always at least a little self-conscious when they dance, but there was nothing like that in the psyche of the Prairie Africans I grew up with. Dancing was like casual conversation for them. They hardly gave it a second thought, but it was unusual if they went more than a few days without it.

I used to watch them. It was the late seventies/early eighties. I remember their joy in dance so clearly. My dad, always eager for others to be having a good time, was often slow to get to the dance floor himself. As the host, it would fall to him to get the music started, or flip the record, or cue up the next cassette. He wasn't a music head and didn't get precious over his tech or anything like that; he just knew what his people liked to hear. And once it was on, he too joined the fray, adding his bouncing step to it, his eyes fixed on his partner, a dance-happy grin on his face; sometimes he would pause his light bob to snap suddenly, or clap once – loudly – at some shift in rhythm or swoop of melody, as though emphasizing to the room – *that's* the point of this song – before goose-necking and skipping back into action. My mother, on the other hand, was a no-nonsense dancer. She took to the floor like she took to all of her projects: with the seriousness of someone intent on doing an excellent job. Make no mistake, excellence in this context means having a good time, so there was smiling involved. But her smiles were intermittent as she regularly focused on getting down to business. Don't let this quirk fool you, though; if there was a moment in which the energy could instinctively ratchet up a notch, my mother was most likely to sense it. She would be the one to let loose a shout of pure happiness, inspiring the others to gear up to that next level.

Paul and Mary, the husband-and-wife team from Trinidad, were our token Africans. There was always something slightly languid in their dance moves, as though they were trying to minimize some of the rhythmic changes that perhaps had been lost between Africa and the Caribbean. They did this regardless of who they danced with, making the Africans appear all the more frenetic and urgent in their moves than they otherwise were. My Uncle Modu and his wife Molly always danced together. Switching partners was a regular affair at these events; in fact, it was often hard to tell who was dancing with whom, so strong was the communal vibe on the dance floor. But Modu and Molly stuck to each other like newlyweds, his eyes soft and dew-filled, her hand always in contact with him, briefly touching an arm or chin or shoulder.

At the centre of it all was Uncle Biola, a large man who loved mixing rum and coke with highlife and soca. I remember him moving in lumbering glee at the centre of the dance floor, his eyes half closed, the sweat pouring from his head. I watched Uncle Biola carefully. Of all the grown-ups he had the least patience with us kids, especially as we entered our teen years. He seemed always exasperated or frustrated with something we did or didn't do, said or didn't say. He was never quite satisfied. If he had a certain look about him – if he had been drinking, say, and was "relaxed" – we had to watch ourselves in his presence. He wasn't a mean man. Far from it. He was actually generous and gregarious. He was simply uncompromising when it came to things that didn't meet his expectations. And one of the things that tested his expectations sorely was the new adolescent attitudes that my age group was adopting.

I was twelve or thirteen at the time, a stifling and impossible age whose impossibility rests precariously on the fact that we can sense *some* sort of freedom exists somewhere out there, nearby, maybe just around the next corner, but we can't see it yet. It is a freedom that beckons from the landscape of our identity. We know there is something that we can become, and that knowledge settles on us like an acrylic sweater, irritating the skin in a way that is impossible to ignore. We experience something similar when we are newly adulted, during our college years, but now we *do* have the freedom to explore that landscape, to try on that sweater and get settled in, to discover *style*. There is still the awkwardness because we are young and have not mastered so much about ourselves. But this awkwardness is different: when we are in college, we are made awkward by too many choices of who to become; when we are adolescents, we are made awkward by too many impositions of who *not* to become. In adolescence this phase is preceded by the innocence of ignorance. But as teenagers, we become aware of ourselves in the world. The sweater we have on was bought by our parents; it doesn't fit. It chafes. It itches. But we have no power of choice to exercise. We can only use our newfound awareness to witness. We become watchers. We watch with a quality that becomes more and more attuned throughout adolescence, eventually turning its scrutinizing energies on itself and culminating in high school, where we become our own incessant police.

To some extent, this policing has never left me. I have never stopped monitoring myself, never stopped finding shortcomings, infractions. It is, perhaps, one of the reasons why I ended up being a poet. Poetry has been my adult self's way of reconciling the contradictions of those internal police I've carried around inside me all of these years. Yes, we all have a version of this police, undoubtedly. But is yours an idiot? Is yours woefully ignorant of the law, but extremely confident of his authority, his decision-making, his judgements? Mine is. Mine is a shameless exemplar of the Dunning–Kruger effect, in which a person's confidence of their competence is inversely proportional to their knowledge of that competency. The less they know about it, the more confidently they rate their expertise in it.

This is my internal police. Officer B. He can make my life miserable, or difficult, but he doesn't care because he doesn't know how little he knows. He is this way because he trained at the academy of Dunning–Kruger. When I was growing up, I was surrounded by white people who unblinkingly claimed to have a greater awareness and a deeper understanding of my racialized experiences than I did. Common occurrences involved white people adamantly claiming that they could detect I was blushing (I wasn't) or that I had an American accent (I didn't), or that I had misinterpreted the nature of a very innocent joke I happened to be the butt of (I hadn't). These corrections were sometimes delivered as biting remonstrations, sometimes as cheerful cajoling. I could never predict which end of the scale I would be tossed on, or which bus I might be tossed under.

I was in the first stages of wearing *that* sweater, but at that point I could not find a proper fit and was struggling with it pulled over my head, unable to distinguish between the actual opening and a sleeve. I was lost in those itchy, acrylic fibres, but like my idiot Officer B., I didn't know that I was entangled in the sleeves of a cheap sweater. This is one of the tragedies of my upbringing: I was so regularly surrounded by confident assertions of my reality that I came to accept those assertions as true. I *knew* I wasn't misinterpreting a "joke," but in the energetic concurrence of everyone around me I stifled my words and in this self-imposed silence the group felt the vindication of their framing. I *knew* I didn't have an

American accent, but in the seemingly random consistency of these encounters, I began to hear something foreign in my own sounds. I *knew* I wasn't blushing, but the general and warm laughter around me, approving of my presence in this one context, was affirming enough to draw a sheepish smile of relief to my face. And in my sheepishness, I wondered if there wasn't perhaps some truth in their exhortations. On one level, I was frustrated; on another level, I was rewarded. On all levels, I remained confounded, suffocating in the synthetic fibres of a sweater I was never going to find my way out of.

One escape route I tried was to become a master of brands. In the eighties, when I was a teenager, brand culture had reached a new zenith of self-awareness. We were Generation X, that generation the rest of you have completely forgotten or quietly wonder, is that an actual generation? Yes, we're an actual generation. (Believe it or not, everyone belongs to an actual generation, even the ones that don't have names.) And if you're uncertain about Gen X, you might find it striking to learn that *that* is precisely Gen X's brand. That *is* the X of Gen X. No, we weren't just docilely wandering our way down the alphabet (have you ever heard of Gen W?); the X is meaningful; the X is symbolic. We are the lost generation, with an amorphous, floating identity. We are disaffected. We jumped off the corporate ladder willingly. Slackers. We have a natural distrust of institutions (with good reason: remember all those Boomers who hated The Man? Well, they *became* The Man). We have no identity, but we identify with irony, cynicism, and counter-culture (we embraced Run-DMC and The Cure). We even ditched Douglas Coupland when he became too popular. While we were busy rejecting everything, something of who we were, as well as the possibilities of who we could become, was crossed out.

When I was old enough and had read enough to think about it, I loved musing about our X as akin to that of Malcolm or Marvin. For them, there is a paradoxical history behind that X, a longstanding and ongoing story of erasure that defines them. In the case of Malcolm X, it was directly tied to American slavery. Generation X in the popular imagination has taken on its own meaning beyond Coupland's original text. In general, the X is understood by my generation as the result of an oversized, self-absorbed generation before us having stolen all of our economic opportunities (we too came of age during recession and in the wake of exploding inflation); having changed the rules of social aspiration (the Jesus freaks and the war objectors became the paragons of corporate conquest); and, having dominated our sensibilities with the sheer excess of their numbers. While these things were true in Coupland's formulation, back then I liked to keep the idea of slavery and historical erasure close at hand. I still do.

As a teenage Gen X-er, before the term Gen X had even been coined, I was steeped in brand culture. This is a result of the swing that Baby Boomers took from shaking their fist at "The Man" to putting their foot to the gas and driving corporate greed to new levels. It's part of what makes cynicism and sarcasm on brand for Gen X. By the time we arrived, television was a ubiquitous fact of life; thus, we were inundated with TV marketing from the time we were children. And although today's generations have been marketed to even more vigorously than we were, they do not experience advertising in the way we did. We could never click on "skip" after ten seconds. We couldn't binge our favourite shows at will, free from *any* advertising. Nor could we have envisioned tools like adblockers, downloadable today for free to anyone who can click a mouse. By no means have the current screen-addled generations had an easier time with marketers; that is not my point. They haven't. Our experiences have been different. Digital marketing today is keyed to the *personal* mobile experience. It assumes that the consumer has more independent choice about what they watch, when, and where. We, on the other hand, were locked into what broadcasters and marketers wanted to show us, and we all watched it together: hit TV shows were a communal affair. I suppose TV back then was like social media today, if social media was just four people who only posted at regularly scheduled times, and there was no way to post back or interact with them. Okay, it was nothing like social media today. Still, it was largely through television that branding entered our homes at new and heightened levels never seen before.

From my perspective as a teenager, marketing in the 1980s was a muscular, masculine affair. It was also aspirant in very particular ways. In the fifties, advertisements might encourage you to buy a home, live in the suburbs, and slowly acquire modern conveniences to fill your home, such as vacuum cleaners, dishwashers, and a sensible, American car to cart your family to weekend picnics. In the eighties, at least to my eyes at the time, ads instructed us to seize a prestige lifestyle that proved society's successful conquests of the fifties. I watched ads filled with brands like Polo by Ralph Lauren. Sperry topsiders. Calvin Klein. Movies featured Italian sports cars. And music videos. Music videos were everywhere, and all of these brands, and more, were regularly brandished in them.

One thing I knew as a teenager was that my African family, and the Afro-Caribbean community through which they negotiated prairie culture, had no clue about the ins and outs of brands like Calvin Klein. I remember having to beg my mom to get me a pair of Levi's 501 jeans, after she had bought me three pairs of Lee jeans because they were on sale. *Lee*?

"What's the difference?" she asked, blinking. A few months later, and after an extensive round of appeals about the difference between the two brands, she came home with a pair of Levi's. I held them up quizzically. The colour was wrong. They were too dark. They weren't stonewashed. I flipped them around only to discover these were some obscure series of Levi's, not the coveted 501s. I didn't even recognize the number: four something. The tab was yellow. *Yellow*? My mother continued with her blank look. Today, I can only imagine the warring emotions she was experiencing beneath that surface of blankness as she looked at her ungrateful, nonsensical, and clearly unhappy Canadian son. From my teen perspective, though, the incident was one of many that confirmed my parents were not reliable when it came to certain social and cultural rules of the day. They didn't understand the currency of brands. I had to be the one to show them. I had to become a master of these brands.

Normally, when my parents announced we were having a get-together with the Prairie Africans that made up our community,

I hardly took notice of the party itself. It was simply a chance to get together with kids who shared so much with me that it was natural for us to think of each other as family. The dynamics were exactly the same. Most of our parents had known each other, or known of each other, in Sierra Leone. Common Sierra Leonean nomenclature involved elders known as "Ma" or "Sa," which is difficult to translate in the Canadian context, but was a term of respect that could, at times, be translated as "sir" or "ma'am," or what Canadians sometimes infer as Uncle or Aunty. It was an approximate concept for us. We didn't use the term, but we thought of each other as cousins.

While my parents had no understanding of the significance of Carl Lewis's flattop, or a Lacoste shirt with collar flipped up, my *cousins* did. A party among the Africans offered me the opportunity to have my mastery reaffirmed by people for whom it *counted*. It might surprise you to learn that the only trouble was that I didn't own any of these brands. Not one.

But I didn't care. I had a plan.

THE THIEF

It was around this time, without any effort or intention, that I developed the power of invincibility. It didn't have to do with superhuman strength or an unnatural impermeability to physical objects. Nor was it the usual sense of invincibility, that Nemean lion's skin that all adolescents shrug into as the marker of youth, its disdain, its ignorance. No, this was a very specific invincibility that I only felt when I was unaccompanied in a store. The origins of this strange superpower actually did emerge in the company of someone else, my closest friend at the time, Gabriel, a wiry, enterprising boy with shaggy blonde hair and an impatient imagination. One day, we were in a drugstore. Gabriel gave me a quick wink, stuffed four bottles of cologne into his backpack and, as my eyes bulged out of my head, strode out of the store with the confidence of someone who knows they are unassailable, who knows no one would even think to stop him on his way out.

And no one did.

I found this episode educational. Gabriel was not captain of the football team or destined to be class president. He was too unorthodox for those things; as you have seen, he was not given to following rules. But he did have charisma, and he had a sort of mysterious energy about him. We nicknamed him "El Greco" for no good reason except that, to us, it seemed congruent with the brand of left-field scheming he was known for, which seemed more dimensioned, more worldly than anything we were used to. It struck us as almost foreign. My mom claimed he had a Charlton Heston chin and giggled in a way that left me stalled, buffering in confusion. (I didn't even know who Charlton Heston was. Later I realized I had been watching him every Easter in my mother's tradition of renting the *Ten Commandments*. I had to admit, there was something Moses-like about Gabriel.) Above all, he was very talkative. He was always coming up with ideas for us to pursue, ideas that seemed outlandish to me: we should get the school to pay us to paint the gym walls; we should convince the drama teacher to let us write the Christmas pageant; we should start a band and organize a battle of the bands with other schools (after we had convinced them to start bands, too). Mostly the plans fizzled out, but there was a lot of energy expelled on the conceiving, planning, and mostly talking about them. Talking was a muscle for Gabriel. It accomplished things for him. He regularly flexed it, exercised it, and like a gangster, sent it out to do his dirty work. Unlike me, Gabriel was completely undaunted by the prospect of using that muscle to rough up any adults in his way. I had been raised by immigrant parents who came from a colonial country, whose upbringing had been mired in Edwardian disciplinarianism decades after Edward VII had died. In their understanding, adults lived in a separate, higher world than children, and the two only mixed if adults either sanctioned or demanded the crossover.

As a result, I had grown up seeing adults as the other team: enemies at worst, irrelevant at best. Not only would it *not* occur to me to start a conversation with an adult, I spent much of my time actively avoiding talking to them at all. But not Gabriel. Gabriel, who was literally a fast talker, would regularly engage them in conversations, barraging them with words, trying to convince them of the worthiness of some scheme of his, trying to persuade them to endorse him in some way, always trying to persuade them. And the only thing that amazed me more than his front-facing hucksterism with adults was the fact that they would sometimes acquiesce. Not often, but the fact that they agreed to *anything* he proposed seemed an incredible feat to me. It was like he had managed to reconfigure the logic of our physical senses, as though suddenly we could now see through our ears or, more accurately, experience a sour stench as sweet. Sure, on paper it might sound positive to encounter floral instead of fart, but do I really want to prove the point by actually taking a deep breath? Of fart? How does this plan work? Despite my confusion, the worst he ever received from adults was an exhausted complaint that they had already said "no" to him and they were tired of hearing him bring it (whatever scheme he'd mentioned) up again and again.

When Gabriel popped those bottles of Polo cologne into his bag, I had a sudden insight into the workings of the world: Gabriel walked out of that store unmolested because he understood himself to be unmolestable. He strode out of the store with the same confidence he showed when he would harangue teachers, or any adult, or any of us, with his latest idea. Gabriel was always convinced that his ideas were achievable, even when they were not, even when they were proven to be unachievable. It never stopped him from trying or from developing the next idea to pursue. I had always thought of this aspect of his personality as thoughtless stubbornness, obtuseness even. But it wasn't that. Gabriel was able to pull off even just a fraction of what he schemed because he fit a script. With his wiry energy, his radiant charisma, his golden-headed brilliance, walking and talking with confidence was *exactly* what the world expected of him. If he happened to stuff his bag with a few unpaid extras along the way, oh well, that was the world's fault for not asking any questions.

The next day I decided I was going back to that same store and taking four more bottles of cologne for myself. I have no idea what crazy impulse made me fixate on going back to the same store, but, actually, that's not true. I do know. I said that Gabriel's shoplifting exploit had revealed something to me. It had: if you follow the right script, you will not be seen. And in my case, the right script, the one I had been following all of my life was exactly that: *I am not seen*. I was Black and Canadian. This double threat was like being the sidekick's sidekick. Nobody sees you.

And nobody did. The next day, I walked out of that store with a bottle of Polo in my backpack. I didn't have the nerve to take four, like Gabriel. But even one bottle of the green elixir bouncing in my backpack was enough to prove the theory. I made it. I wasn't seen. I was invincible.

THE TRIBES

It was not such an unreasonable conclusion. At school, I had no tribe. My true tribe was poets. But I didn't know that yet and, anyway, there was no such tribe in any school in my experience of the eighties. Besides, I didn't know that poetry was a calling. I didn't know who my tribe was at all. Honestly, nobody did. I'm not suggesting that I was friendless or alienated. I did feel a certain amount of alienation, but this was on a general, racialized level from society. On an individual level, I had lots of friends. I could even, to a limited extent, have been considered popular. But that was more a consequence of being friends with the kids who were truly popular. I was among the in-crowd, but I didn't feel *in* it.

Part of this, I think, had to do with my ambiguous tribal affiliations. I was most readily identified as a "jock." This is because I happened to be athletic and was often encouraged and successful in my athleticism. In fact, it was a regular occurrence for me to have coaches of all sorts — but especially basketball coaches — chasing me down in the hallway to recruit me for the school team. This they did without knowing anything about me other than what they saw at face value in front of them. I can only imagine the electric thrill these coaches felt when they first saw me wandering the hallway, or glimpsed me through the open door of a class I was sitting in. There are surprisingly few vocations in which the structures of your profession are so readily available to symbolic meaning. This is why shows like *Law and Order* have so many franchise spinoffs: cops, lawyers, and doctors offer up symbols of good/bad and life/death with such naked readiness that Hollywood can hardly resist them. So, too, does a Black boy shine with symbolism to a basketball coach drowning in white wannabes. Too bad for them I am a terrible basketball player; eventually, the sad truth always outed itself. Too bad for me that none of my academic teachers ever thought to pursue me with even half of the enthusiasm demonstrated by every single coach I ever crossed paths with as a student. Also, too bad for me that in most other sports I did excel. Once again, Officer B., my internal police officer, directed me not to question things or he would have to punish me. Surely I could see how successful I was as an athlete? Doesn't it follow that I was being pursued because I had a natural gift? Wasn't it logical? Mollified, I had to concede to Officer B.'s logic. I also had to quash the feelings of dislike I had for many of the sports I competed in; I had to quash the deep despair I felt at the attention I craved from my academic teachers but hardly ever received, the invisibility that, in this case, worked against me.

Occasionally, though, other tribes of teenagers would see me. There was a brand of black-clad, eye-lined scowlers who were not quite Goths yet, but who pioneered some of their tendencies. They listened to The Cure, and The Smiths, and Depeche Mode. They cast glowering looks about them. They held disdain for everything commercial or popular. They were the first to smoke. At the time, the name we gave these proto-Goths was straightforward, self-explanatory even: Alternatives. And to many of us they were just like the Alt key on keyboards that had yet to fully make their entrance in schools: they were there; everyone saw them plainly belonging to the general environment; but no one really knew what they did or why. They seemed irritated, but it was unclear at what. They also seemed convinced of their superiority, but no one fully understood what it was based on. Occasionally, though, they actually saw me. In fact, we saw each other. For the most part, the Alt key does actually do nothing. But when you combine it with other keys, it turns out it does a lot. The proto-Goth, Alternatives' super-combination power was England. Their love of Morrissey and Robert Smith immersed them in a particular corner of British culture and, as it turns out, when they immersed their heads below the surface line of 1980s Britain, they found me already sitting there.

My presence there was an accident of history. This accident, though, is shared by a very large number of people: whole populations that were impacted by British colonialism. Many countries were victimized by colonialism, but some countries were impacted differently than others. (Countries like Canada were colonized, but as favoured family members. Countries in Africa, Asia, and the Caribbean were colonized as unruly problems.) While Australia, New Zealand, and Canada are understood to have "shared values" with Britain, the unruly populations of Africa, Asia, and the Caribbean are understood to need a certain character stamped on them: British education, Christian religion, the English language, and many other Western cultural traditions were imposed as the standard to attain. My parents learned "God Save the King," spoke English, and wore public school uniforms at school. None of these things would look out of place in England. Indeed, it was intentional: colonialism=clone-ialism. Colonial offshoots were viewed as (lesser) versions of the U.K. itself. My father's undergraduate degree was earned at Fourah Bay College in Freetown, but qualified as an equivalent to Durham University, which – he never failed to point out – is England's #3 university (or, in his words, *second* only to Oxbridge). After high school, my mother attended school in Bristol, where she ended up living for six years. These connections were not natural; they were colonial, but they were *accessed* naturally, with ease; it was actually hard to avoid them.

As the child of immigrants, I often saw my parents' engagements with Canadian culture as awkward, sometimes nonsensical. My dad wasn't engrossed with *Hockey Night in Canada*, like many of my friends' fathers were. My mother didn't bake chocolate chip cookies on any sunny Saturday morning: she fried plantain chips or cooked up pots of *plasas* and *fufu*. To my relief, neither of my parents had strong African accents, but white people were often eager to point out even the mildest departures of the tongue, the slightest variations. The worst, for me, was the sabotages they regularly dropped into my life in the form of words. Though I had no discernible (foreign) accent, white people were regularly trying to detect one in me. When that failed, they would exult at some of my word choices. My lexicon, quite innocently, included references to car boots (trunks), chesterfields (sofas), vests (tank tops), brollies (umbrellas), etc. When my dad wanted to encourage me, he would use words like, "good show" or "jolly good." He often referred to my friends as "lads" or "chaps." I knew words like "Scousers" and "Geordies" long before I ever knew what or who they referred to. I knew there was some sort of divide between North and South England, as well as North and South London, though I had never experienced nor understood their particular distinctions.

Occasionally, I would refer to these contexts or use their associated words with other Canadians. I did it unselfconsciously, unthinkingly. But the reaction was like I had set off a bomb in an empty field. Or like I had walked out in public wearing no pants. The confusion it elicited ranged from snarl-lipped disdain to open-mouthed blinking. Sometimes I was mocked, sometimes corrected. Sometimes I was harangued, sometimes lectured. In all cases, my internal response was a combination of shame, frustration, and resentment toward my parents, who had unwittingly lined the pathways of my childhood with these unexpected explosives.

I received a different treatment from the Alternatives. These proto-Goths regarded my cultural gaffs with respect. It was as though I, as an outsider, was confirming the legitimacy of this other, yearned-for world, reflected in the music they revered. Yet, it was a world they had no direct way of accessing through the casual realities of their everyday Canadian lives. In this context, my otherness, my unbelonging *and* my everdayness was, paradoxically, an asset. It did no good for one of their own to affirm British culture in 1980s Western Canada, but when some rando non-Goth could hear the Sex Pistols's "God Save the Queen" and *get* the reference, they were rhapsodic. For a moment, we could serve each other by looking across some unnamed teenage divide and *see* each other. They didn't look that strange to me when I connected them to a world that was regularly referenced in my home, a world where I had actually spent one epic summer visiting my cousins, learning the difference between an Essex accent and a Suffolk accent. The Alternatives and I could look across the divide and see each other, but not for who we actually were; rather, we saw what we needed to see to consolidate our outsider identity. They needed me to recognize the Britishness in them; I needed them to redeem my parents' acts of sabotage, remove the fault I felt for possessing a familiarity with something foreign. In this way, we saw each other though we saw past each other. There was an affirmation of sorts, but it didn't answer my fundamental doubts of belonging. I was still P.D. Eastman's hapless hatchling, circling his surroundings, wandering from group to group, never resting, never rested. "Are you my tribe? Are you my tribe?" The jocks gave me an emphatic *yes* because I looked the part. The preps gave me an emphatic shrug. The Alternatives gave me a distant nod. If I was able to skirt the boundaries of all of these groups it is because none of them could actually see me. Maybe it was an of advantage of sorts, a kind of power that allowed me to move between these groups. But if it was, that power, like so much of my life, was a feature of being unseen. Truthfully, I didn't have a tribe.

THE MARKETPLACE

"Are you my tribe?" is a question that would have confused my parents. The whole context of responses it demands would have made no sense to them. Growing up in Freetown, Sierra Leone is like growing up in the world's largest rumour mill. If you didn't know someone personally, you knew their family, or you knew someone who knew their family. Six degrees of separation would have struck them as overdoing it. To get beyond *three* degrees you had to be in another country or be dead. When I was ten, we went to Freetown for a few weeks in the summer and I came face to face with this phenomenon. During the visit, I was shuffled between my parents from place to place, visiting a myriad of relatives and family friends who were extremely keen to meet the "American" boy, but whom I only knew vaguely through stories I had heard throughout my childhood. After a particularly long afternoon of visiting, my father, looking gaunt and peeved, suggested we detour through a local market before heading to the next set of welcomers. The marketplace was pure chaos to me. It was nothing like the supermarket I was familiar with in Canada and more like a soccer game on a pitch overcrowded with fans and players alike. Everything seemed both excited and out of place. Hawkers sang out with lusty energy as we walked by their wares. I recognized one boy and his singsong melody of "ka-ro-zin-ye," which I was getting used to hearing outside my window every morning as I woke up. But my father shook his head, "that's someone else, not him." Half the time there was so much going on I couldn't tell which side was for shoppers and which side was for vendors. We struck up conversations with many different people as we ambled through, but we didn't buy anything.

Finally, my dad said that we'd better get going or someone was going to wonder where we were. When we got to the next house, we were greeted with warm enthusiasm, when all of a sudden the mood took a sudden swing in the wrong direction.

"Eh, *bo*, Chini!" My dad's childhood friend complained to him. "I hear you were in the market talking to that kerosene boy when you should have been here enjoying a nice drink with me! Why did you make me wait like that? Aren't I your good friend?"

A little bit of that gaunt look haunted my dad's looks again, but he is an amiable man by nature and so he shook it off with a grin and playfully begged forgiveness.

"Bertrand wanted to see the market," he said, improvising. "I couldn't say no to him. He just wants to see what he's been missing all these years."

I was shocked. First, my dad was essentially lying to his friend, right in front of my face. This was something I had never known my father to do at all. In fact, he was nearly apoplectic if he even so much as sniffed an untruth coming from my direction. The other thing that shocked me was the fact that everyone seemed to know exactly where we had been even though we had been spontaneous and had not met anyone we knew. I suspected the kerosene boy, who had been invoked by my dad's friend. And then I wondered at the fact that my father may have lied *twice* to me within an hour. But the more I thought about it, the less sense it made. The kerosene seller that I heard from my bedroom window every morning had no personal relationship with our household, as far as I could tell. We didn't even buy kerosene from him. He just wandered through the neighbourhood singing his song; he never stopped at our place. No, it wasn't him. Somehow, through the warren of underground communication that is Krio society, word had spread about our whereabouts, and, at least to everyone who mattered to us, there was nothing secret about our secret detour. This is what happens in a community like the Krios of Freetown. This is what happens when three degrees of separation is the norm. There is no tribe because *everyone* is in the tribe.

But I didn't grow up in Freetown. I didn't experience this kind of community, marked by constant relating, a ubiquitous belonging that appeared to impact my father in a surprising way. Generally a jovial and patient man, he appeared exasperated, constricted by the pervasiveness of his Krio upbringing. Freetown, to him, was anything but free. It was more hometown helicopter-parent than supportive network. But my perspective was completely different. My yearnings were wholly governed by growing up in a place that refused to acknowledge me as a natural, normal member of the community. Nobody watched over me from afar, as they did me and my dad as we roamed the marketplace, my father feigning interest in this and that. When I was noticed, if I was noticed, it was with eye-popping horror or dehumanizing curiosity. For me, *belonging* was a shield against that inhumanity. It was the thing I longed for almost more than anything else. To this day, I think it marks me. At different points in my life I have consistently wanted to join bands or be on a team or form a collective or simply *participate* in some kind of group endeavour. I have a group chat that I'm on with some of my writer friends and I have to hold myself back from being that guy who comments *all* the time. For all the pain I endured in my youth for being categorized and defined in particular ways, the result is that I *love* being in specifically categorized company: me and my people.

Although I felt these yearnings as a teenager, I didn't realize I had them at the time. I just felt – like most teenagers for their diversely trivial and profound reasons – painfully awkward. I received a certain recognition from the neo-Goths, but it was clear to them and me that they weren't my tribe. If anything, I was caught between two other tribes: the jocks and the preps. I was associated with jocks for the obvious reason of my perceived athleticism, as I mentioned above. But I wasn't really a jock. I wasn't really into sports; I wasn't obsessive or even competitive about them. I hardly followed any pro sports teams. I didn't wear the gear. I really didn't care that much. To be honest, when I got out of high school, I stopped playing sports altogether and didn't miss them one bit. In fact, I've long since come to realize that for years

I had been living the bizarre situation of being an athlete who didn't enjoy athleting. This is why I say I was associated with jocks, rather than I was a jock.

The same can be said of the preps. I wasn't really considered preppy, but by dint of the schools I went to in Calgary (Elboya and Western), preppiness was the dominant culture and so by default I was immersed in it. Many of my friends *were* preps and so, again, I was associated by default. But nobody actually saw me as legitimately preppy. Consider Alfonso Ribeiro's character, Carlton, in *The Fresh Prince of Bel-Air*. He is full-on preppy. He favours cardigans and topsiders with no socks. He drapes a sweater around his shoulders and ties it kitchly in front. He uses his white voice *all* the time. He dances from the knees, bopping up and down, giving his fingers a vigorous snap *on* the beat, his head careening from side to side, his face plastered with a careless grin. He is meant to be funny, and the joke is clear. Carlton's Blackness is an anomaly: preppiness is akin to whiteness, and a Black man jaunting about in the trappings of whiteness is a laughing matter. If wealthy Carlton, in the heart of a fashionable Los Angeles suburb, is incapable of hitting the mark without being a joke, I was never going to fly as anything authentically preppy in prairie-town Alberta. The only reason I got away with the association is because it was the default culture of my environs. As the old joke goes, it's the fish who asks, "What the hell is water?" and preppiness was the water of my school environment. We plunged into *Pretty in Pink*; we washed up along Calvin Klein; we steeped in Sperry Topsiders.

To the same extent that Goths disdained brands and commercialism of all sorts, brand culture was the spine that erected preppiness. This is why my natural inclination was to become something of a brand expert. I didn't feel seen and so I tried to counter my invisibility with the trappings of visible commercialism. All of us were susceptible to the lure of these brands, though. It wasn't just me and my racialized inner turmoils. A national parallel was taking place that simply validated those feelings. The 1980s was an era of intense commodification because cable TV suddenly became a thing and ushered it into our unsuspecting lives. In some ways, cable TV of the eighties was like social media of the twenty-first century. It gave us access to a meaningful world so that we didn't have to feel so backwoods, so provincial, so unseen.

The threat of Americanization is a fixture of Canadian identity, and to many this was one more avenue toward its inevitable arrival since hoards of kids seemed to be lapping it up without a second thought. Once, my social studies teacher, in an attempt to demonstrate the inherent value of our Canadianness, spontaneously polled the class as to how many of us would be okay with becoming a part of the U.S. A slight majority of us was okay with that. His eyes popped out of his head. It was the last thing he had expected. He had instinctively called for the poll as a reflexive gesture of patriotism: Canadians often struggle with expressions of patriotism, but the one thing we have all tacitly agreed on is that we are *not* American. As I write this, we are well into our anti-Trump, elbows-up national campaign of 2025, and it has been so wholeheartedly adopted because it scratches that most uncategorical itch on the spine of Canadian patriotism. The easiest thing a Canadian can do to get on the same page with any other Canadian is assert our moral (etc., etc.) superiority to the U.S. What my social studies teacher couldn't have known is that cable TV imported teenage trends, popular culture, the *cool* of adolescence we all wanted so badly to inhabit, and it confirmed to us that none of it was located in Canada. We didn't actually want to be Americans. We just wanted to wear Jordache and Lacoste and cut class like Ferris Bueller and live our lives like a music video. We wanted to be seen.

To a certain extent, too, Canada has always wanted to be seen. We are caught between the past of our British heritage and the present of our North American modernity. It is hard to stand out when your anchoring points feel adrift; it is hard to stand out when your drama reads like someone else's script. So it wasn't only naive consumerism that drove us to seek out America. It was also our desire *not* to be America. How strange that this world I was growing up in, so different from the one of my parents' childhoods, created a pathway for me to understand my African identity. Even stranger that it was my African identity, in a shared rhythm with Alberta, in turn that showed me how strongly I am connected to the Prairies. It took me years to learn the intricacies of this rhythmic interplay, years to discern the grand right and left of it all. I feel a little dismayed by that. But it was impossible for me to see it back then. I was, after all, only a boy.

BOY

A few days after I stole the bottle of Polo from that same shelf Gabriel had targeted, I found myself warily watching my Uncle Biola at the party my parents were throwing for his wife. Uncle Biola was a stubborn man. In West Africa, there is a type of man that is sometimes called a "real" African man. He is traditional in an uncompromising and self-certain way. He is a man of few words, guided by his physicality. No matter how ridiculous or impossible his version of the world is, he demands acquiescence to it and punishes those who fail to uphold this vision. If you are familiar with classic African literature, then you know that Okonkwo, the protagonist of Chinua Achebe's seminal novel, *Things Fall Apart*, is a "real" African man. In fact, the novel's tragic achievement is that he is such a man in a world that is losing its hold on tradition. You are frustrated by Okonkwo's inflexibility but also devastated at his thorough demise. A part of you wishes that he could have been more adaptable and a part of you wishes the world could have been more forgiving.

My Uncle Biola was a modern type of a "real" African man. By this I mean, he might have been the complete article had he stayed in Sierra Leone, but like so many people of my parents' generation, he left a state of optimism and burgeoning national pride simply to further his education in the West, never suspecting the downward turn his country would tragically take. In his case, he came to Canada with my aunt, whose name is also Biola, and they started their new life, literally, in the West.

This shift in geography shifted something of what his character was capable of achieving as a "real" African man. Obviously, in Canada, you cannot smack a child over the head with a wooden crate, as happened to another uncle of mine who was too slow to respond to his teacher's request to move the crate from a nearby table. You cannot scream at a passenger in your car – who is in your car because it is a cab and you are the cab driver – when that passenger apparently slams the car door too forcefully for your liking.

And, obviously, I have no idea if Uncle Biola would have done anything like these things if they had stayed in Sierra Leone. But I do know that he exercised his own version of African manhood in Alberta. If the fitful weather demanded we protect ourselves, he would roll up his sleeves and saunter outside into the February cold with no winter gear on at all. He would shrug at our exasperated looks, our eyes popping with frustration and devastation. He favoured seventies shirts with large collars and bold patterns in thin polyester at all times of the year. He booted up in brown suede Chelsea slip-ons with black gussets on the side, snow or no snow. Truthfully, he was dapper. He claimed not to feel the cold at all. Maybe he was too cool for the cold.

He was a headstrong man, tall, but thickly built with an enormous belly. He had an insatiable energy. Like many Africans, our parents loved to get together, drink a little and dance a lot. Uncle Biola was ever present, shouting stories at the top of his lungs, drinking a lot, and dancing even more. When Jheri curls became a thing in the eighties, he was first to jump on the bandwagon and the last to reluctantly step off of it a couple of decades later. I have a lasting image of him in the centre of the dance floor (our living room), holding a rum and coke aloft, singing loudly to Debbie Harry's "The Tide is High," his Jheri curls collapsed against his forehead, sweat pouring down his face, the world spinning in helpless rhythm around his gravitational glee.

But he was diabetic and he was careless with his medication, especially if he was having a good time. At times, my Aunty Biola (who went by Sarah in the wider world) was at her wits' end with him. No pushover herself, her urgings for him to take his medication would escalate to desperation and then, quickly, from there, all-out explosion. It was during these times that I would get glimpses of what Uncle Biola, as a "real" African man, might have been like. His eyes, already red, narrowed and his breath came out stertorously, painfully loud. Aunty Biola was like a welterweight boxer circling him with her words, lighter than his, but with insistent, relentless jabbing. Uncle Biola absorbed it all, like the heavyweight he was, until he could tolerate it no longer. Then a low moan, the sound of agitated cattle, would rumble from his depths. Something in his features would change, and the whole evening's atmosphere, which had been compelled to circle his luminous energy, would shift to some unknown, precarious territory.

I was about twelve years old. This sight of my uncle and the transformation it demanded of the room struck me in an unexpected way: I *wanted* the shift. I wanted my Uncle to complete his transformation. I wanted to see him explode from his body and emerge as a "real" African man. Far from sensing anything dangerous or unhinged in the encounter, I saw it as an opportunity to look into a window that had been closed to me all my life.

Although I was born in Sierra Leone, I was raised here and had no lived memories of the community I was meant to be from. This was a double-edged sword for me as, on the one hand, I was always susceptible to white Canadians denying the legitimacy of my Canadianness, and, on the other, I was teased by my parents for being, what they called, "Canada Boy." Though I was too young to understand it, let alone do anything about it, asserting the validity of one side of my identity always risked jeopardizing the other in a push and pull that left me feeling adrift between two cultural masses, unable to lock into orbit around either one. In this suspended uncertainty, I was unconsciously drawn to moments that were both capable of confirming my identity and ruthlessly tearing apart its fabric at the same time.

Uncle Biola's cornered look, his animal growl, promised me a view into my African background that I knew was an authentic version I otherwise had no access to. It would confirm all of the stories that I had heard from my parents' generation, stories that were, I see now, meant as warnings of what was possible for an "authentically" Sierra Leonean lived experience. In my parents' view, a world that allowed you to punish a child because they were too loud or too slow or too brash or too hasty or too quiet was wrong. I didn't hear their warning. Maybe I thought there was an "authentic" possibility for *me* to live out as well. Maybe I felt a "real" African man could counter the denials from white Canadians who, it seemed to me, were denying my right to occupy the same spaces as them, with the same legitimacy. I don't know. I only know that I wasn't afraid or uncertain of Uncle Biola's simmering gaze. I only know that I wanted to stoke the fire.

At that moment, the rest of the party-goers intervened, circling Uncle Biola, gripping him and chastising him in Krio, trying to laugh it off. "*Bo*," they said, "come on, just take your medicine and let's dance!" They cajoled him until a sheepish smile crept onto his face. He downed his pills with a gulp whiskey and shouted for Boney M. The party roared back to life. The dancing lasted all night long.

In Krio, *bo* is a complex word. In one sense, it has roots with and is very similar to the English word *boy*. To my Canadian ears it sounded like the diminutive of the word *bɔbɔ*, which can literally mean boy. This turns out not to be true. When Uncle Biola was being entreated by the other party-goers to calm down and take his medicine, he was not being called a "boy." When *bo* is being deployed in this sense, "Eh *bo*, take your medicine so we can all dance again," it is somewhere between a gesture of familiarity and a rhetorical expletive. In English, we might say something like, "Hey man, chill," or "C'mon, bro," and the "man" or "bro" in this context evokes a familiarity ("C'mon man/bro, we're on the same team here") but it can also simply be an expletive, empty of true grammatical meaning. And for me, as a youngster, floating behind the meanings and non-meaning of *bo*, somewhere in the distance, was the historical spectre of "boy." One of the tools of empowerment I stumbled on when I was younger was challenging white people who addressed me using the term "boy." At some point, I discovered that this would unbalance them from their usual perch of confidence and control over my status in what they perceived of as their world. Without warning, I would lash out with "Who you calling '*boy*'?" and they would be startled into slack-jawed stammering or wide-eyed silence. No matter that it had been said to me in innocence or endearment even, they felt the electricity of my reprimand and they were knocked from their perch. Truthfully, I didn't fully understand why this phrase held the power it did. But like anyone whose general situation makes them feel hungry for power, when I found this tool of power, I honed and wielded it without hesitation. I didn't care that I didn't fully understand it.

The same could be said for me and the word *bo*. My inclination to see "boy" in *bo* was a miscue. The word can be a tricky invocation for the uninitiated, non-Krio speaker, and I was a halfling Krio speaker at best. But for Uncle Biola and the rest of my parents' generation, even displaced as they were in Canada's English, all of these complexities were expressed and understood effortlessly. So, when Uncle Biola was called *bo*, he knew what company he was in. And, actually, whatever precarity I might have picked up on as a twelve-year-old, whatever doubts I may have had about Uncle Biola's potential transformation into a true, "real" African man, more likely had to do with my Canadian clumsiness with the language and with the culture as a whole. He knew how to respond. Maybe there was never a danger of anything else happening.

This, too, I like to think of as Uncle Biola's brand. He was as much at home at the centre of an African party, teetering on some edge, as he was gossiping about the Calgary Flames's latest travail with a random stranger at the bus stop. It was as though he didn't notice the change of setting. This was part of the modern character of him being a "real" African man. He was stubbornly, exactly the same man whether he was walking through a street market on Kroo Town Road in Freetown or helping to jump start someone's car in the heart of an Albertan February. Even his outfits remained the same. World be damned.

Nothing marks my parents' generation as transitional more than where they gave birth to my generation. Some, who came to Canada just before my parents, had all of their children in Freetown and then moved. Some, like my Uncle Biola, came to Canada and then had all of their children. But most split their children's birthplaces between the two countries. My parents, who only managed to eke out two kids, are exemplary of this. I was born in Sierra Leone while my younger sister was born in Edmonton.

My sister is the same age as Uncle Biola's kids. Because I am older, I remember when Uncle Biola's middle child was born. I was maybe eleven years old, so my perspective is limited, but I have one clear memory. Uncle Biola, ever full of impulsive, original ideas, had decided to order a cake for his wife to celebrate the birth she had just laboured through. He placed a phone order with Woodwards bakery for the cake to be iced with his new son's name.

There was a pause over the phone and you could almost see a quizzical eyebrow being raised: "Happy Birthday Jersey?" she asked, confused.

"No, no," Uncle Biola shouted, "Happy Birthday Georgie."

Another pause: "Jody?"

"Georgie," my uncle roared, "Georgie!"

I don't know how the entire conversation went. I'm quite sure that if Uncle Biola was tentatively asked to spell Georgie, he would have categorically refused. After all, in his world, if you don't know how to spell Georgie, that's your problem. In Uncle Biola's world, there was very little need for questions at all. The sun rose in the east and set in the west. Pademba Road was as logical a place to buy cassava leaves as West Edmonton Mall. Wide-collared, pattern-splayed polyester shirts wore as well in the middle of summer as in the middle of winter. If you can't spell Georgie, you're an idiot.

I wasn't there, but I remember hearing stories of my Aunty Biola, waking up harried and exhausted in her hospital bed, my uncle's wide-toothed smile, holding out a cake with a single candle: "Happy Birthday Judgy." This story garnered widespread hilarity from the Sierra Leonean community. But it peeved me. In part, this difference in our responses was a demonstration of a distance between us. A distance I hated. For so much of my life I was lost in space, drifting in orbit between the gravitational pull of my Sierra Leonean and Canadian twin stars. I would approach one, suddenly finding myself careening out of control as the force of its mass slingshot me right past it headlong toward the other star, only to be flung right back to the first in a dizzying star dusted-loop of infinity.

Something as innocuous as a shared joke could demonstrate me to be flailing farther and farther away from the group I wanted to be attached to. Because I was always trying to stay in the orbit of one of the stars, being rejected by its gravity inevitably evinced *feelings* of rejection. And the closer I approached my teen years, the more my go-to emotion for coping was courting with anger.

It is with some shame that I admit that many of the sources of anger in my life at the time were the very things from which I sought a sense of belonging. Uncle Biola was one such source. I loved many things about him: his maverick sense of fashion; his inflexible expectations; his unfaltering joy at parties. But one thing I could not stomach was his persistent, impenetrable accent. Worse, I felt burdened and embarrassed by it. Even after decades of living in Canada, Uncle Biola sounded like he had just arrived and was doggedly, if still gamefully, attending part-time weekend lessons in English.

It pained me to hear him talking to white Canadians, especially those I knew, especially my friends. It felt akin to having something very personal, very private exposed to the world for ridicule. He sounded reduced and boyish to me. In those moments, I was hyper-aware of how he was being perceived, how his unflinching character was reduced to an animalness, how his maverick impulses seemed to betray us all. It never occurred to me to question my own feelings. It never occurred to me that I might be the one who was the betrayer.

Really, it was insane: I wanted him to be a "real" African man and I was proud of all the ways in which he stood out from the common crowd; at the same time, when it came to his speech anyway, I was ashamed that this very same Africanness was on display. The boyishness in the etymology of *bɔbɔ* seemed emphasized to me in these moments. His mouth's hopeless contortions around simple words were in my mind not just the public sign of incompetency, but of immaturity, an unfinished intelligence, an underdeveloped understanding of certain basics.

When I was older, he took me to his favourite car wash to show me the ropes of caring for my first car. Today, this is one of my fondest memories of him. He loved cars and he loved caring for them. It is no coincidence that his many and sudden jaunts into wild winter weather, without appropriate clothing, were to rescue someone having a car "situation," like a flat tire or a dead battery. On this hot summer day, he took me to the Bubble Mart like it was a rite of passage. He led me through the ceremony of hand-washing, drying and waxing. I learned all of the magic tricks of various kinds of chamois. He introduced me to his moustached, muscle-car friends. Throughout it all, just like our family parties, full of drink and dance, Uncle Biola was the magnet at the centre of the day's energy. Everyone swirled around him, indulging in greetings, sharing stories, asking his advice. He absorbed it all, smoothly stepping toward and turning from person to person, swirling in graceful veronicas, like an age-old matador calmly deflecting the charging bull, using its energy as a source of creativity, his dance, his art.

Today, I cherish this memory. But for years, it raised my ire, especially as a teenager, for the simple reason that when he introduced me, he called me "Bat." When I was younger and being buffeted about by the opposing gravitational wells of the twin stars that raised me, I was self-conscious about the name Bertrand. No sooner had I expelled its two syllables than people scrunched their eyes and raised a lip in a snarl of confusion: "Burr – what?" I very quickly developed the habit of shortening my name to Bert, a simple and single syllable that was, I was sure, as harmless and familiar as the cone-headed, yellow Muppet everyone knew.

But in my Uncle Biola's mouth, this simple syllable was transformed into a simplistic shadow, a caricature of itself. For all of my inward contortions over these varying expressions of my name — of who I was — it turns out that even this embarrassment over my beloved uncle's way with words was yet another pathway, another trail, that would eventually lead me to connect my African family history with the Prairies' historical legacy.

PART 2

SECRET LANGUAGES

THE SECRET LANGUAGE OF BLACK HISTORY

Whose history can I claim? Whose stories apply to me, help to build my own? I am an African in Alberta. I am also an Albertan out of Africa. Cheryl Foggo, the undisputed doyenne of the historical and ongoing narrative of the Black Prairies, has often talked about the importance of discovering John Ware in her childhood. Understandably, as residents of the "Last Best West," she and her brother were fanatics of all things cowboys when they were young and had, of course, heard of John Ware. Yet, they had been completely unaware of Ware's Blackness until Richard Foggo came face to face with it on a school trip to the local museum. This revelation shattered their previous assumptions of what or who a cowboy is and kicked off what might be thought of as Cheryl's lifelong love affair with the magnificent figure of John Ware, Black cowboy.

I completely relate to this form of ambivalent reconciliation with history. On the one hand, discovering that an important historical figure — who contributed to the makeup and character of the wider province — was Black, was an exhilarating, affirming experience. On the other hand, the recognition that such a figure even existed in our history and yet had been denied the prominence he so obviously deserved, was yet another reminder of the relegated status Blackness holds in this province — this country — by default. For Cheryl, whose family story is a living monument to the central place of Black communities in the pioneering history of the Prairies, the response to this default relegating is obvious: counter it as vigorously as possible with writing, with films, with public talks, with creative and intellectual works of all sorts embodied with her own pointed acuity and magnanimous patience.

For Cheryl, this response is a straightforward one, perhaps, because her family history aligns with the formative colonial history of the Prairies. Mine doesn't. That is, it doesn't align with the history that is seen as emblematic of Alberta's essence. I am referring to wheat and oil, farmers and homesteaders, cowboys and fur traders. These are the incipient trajectories of our province that launched Alberta into the tax-averse, lone-wolf, MAGA-tempted maverick it is today. And my family story does not fit any of those trajectories. But John Ware does appeal to me. Like Cheryl, I had a revelatory moment of discovering his Blackness and questioning the so-called legitimacy of what I had been taught before. When I think of my family story, I think of Uncle Biola howling at *Hockey Night in Canada* as his beloved Flames carve out an unlikely victory; I think of the Prairie Africans spinning something new out of Debbie Harry's reggae inflections and Paul Simon's claims on Zulu culture, defying gravity on the dance floor. Like my family — like all of the trajectories of Alberta's colonial history — John Ware came from elsewhere. I like to think that there is something common in our Blackness, an entity that was — and still is — imposed on us. And as a result, we have had to make something common with it.

I think the difference between me and Cheryl is that I never identified with cowboys because I never felt I could. It was so obviously a binary world of white vs. other, good vs. bad, cowboy vs.

"Indian," winner vs. loser, and it was so obvious which side of the equation I was meant to stand on regardless of the actual realities of my being, or the facts of history, or laws of the physical universe for that matter. Cheryl's family *is* Albertan and so the fact of this equation of always diminishing returns was, eventually, something she could challenge. But my family story, and its accompanying history, was from a completely different part of the world and seemed to have no connections to this one. Think, then, of my surprise when I one day realized that I had been wrong all of these years. That all of us had been wrong all of these years. That Blackness that I instinctively felt linked us in communal ways in the present also has direct connections to a shared historical past. One of the ways that I came to discover this truth is through my own exploration of cowboy culture.

One thing that you learn very quickly when you do historical research, is that there is always far more beneath the known surface than you could have suspected. If you come across the hint of an unusuality, you are almost guaranteed to find an entire community and longstanding histories underpinning that first hint, if you only keep looking. John Ware immediately proves this point. He is commonly narrated as a lone Black figure conquering the white ranching world. But what is often overlooked is that many of the stories told about him also refer to other Black people who he interacted with. For one thing, John Ware was married and had children. This was possible because an entire family of Black people — the Lewises — had moved from Toronto and had been living near Shepard just south of Calgary when Ware met one of their daughters. Indeed, one of the stories of their courtship includes a double date with *another* Black couple and involves a startling event in which the democrat they were travelling in was struck by lightning, killing the horses and giving the occupants a huge scare. There is another example in Grant MacEwan's popular biography, *John Ware's Cow Country*, in which MacEwan identifies Pete Smith, a Black friend, who comes to help when Ware had his fatal accident, his horse tripping on a badger hole and falling on top of him. It is also plainly documented that he worked with other Black cowboys, including Green Walters, a popular and industrious hustler who managed to pull off a number of ranching roles.

Grant MacEwan also gets in on this act of normalizing Black presence on the Prairies as unusual. MacEwan's biography of John Ware is considered the authoritative account of Ware's life. It was, however, written decades after Ware died and relies on oral accounts recalled from old-timers' memories as much as documented evidence. MacEwan's goal as a historian was to create a narrative as enjoyable and compelling as a novel, or what he might refer to as a good yarn.[1] If some facts fall by the wayside for the sake of an absorbing drama, the payoff is worth it for MacEwan. Needless to say, the accuracy of *John Ware's Cow Country* is questionable in places. Nevertheless, MacEwan can't help representing Black belonging with that particularly ambivalent understanding that is so commonly assumed here on the Prairies.

---

1 For more on MacEwan's priority on narrative see Max Foran, ed., *Grant MacEwan's Journals* (Edmonton, AB: Lone Pine Publishing, 1986), 5.

At one point in the text, he has John Ware act as an ambassador of the frontier to some upper-class English visitors who had come to view their investment and get a taste of the "Wild West." The guests are out of their depth and reveal their general incompetence to the point that Ware must actually rescue one "Lord Harold" out of a riding incident. The local horsemen are peeved by the Englishman's arrogance, but Ware holds his tongue in an act of gentlemanly reserve. The message is clear: the West accommodates all sorts of disparate characters, but it is no place for the likes of "Earls" and "Lords." In this sense, MacEwan has made Ware exemplary of Western belonging: he is lowborn, unrefined, hard-working, as well as both self-made and selfless; this makes him more of a gentleman than the actual gentlemen. For MacEwan, there is no higher indication of someone who belongs to the Prairie West.[2]

But then, on the very next page, Ware's position as a figure of unquestionable belonging is suddenly upended. While leading his horse back to the stable, he is surprised to come across a young, Black man napping nearby. He wakes him and learns the youth is from "Dixie," the American South. "Man," Ware exclaims, "you're sure a long way from home!"[3] Only moments before, MacEwan had held Ware up as a paragon of the West, as a Black man who is at home on the Canadian prairie. Yet, it appears that *Blackness* itself on the prairie remains the sign of uprootedness, of displacement,

2 Three key indicators for MacEwan are honesty, friendliness, and resourcefulness. See Grant MacEwan, *John Ware's Cow Country* (Edmonton: Institute of Applied Art, Ltd., 1960), 256.

3 MacEwan, *John Ware's Cow Country*, 125.

of not-home. Here is the crux of ambivalent Black belonging. As a cowboy in Alberta, John Ware is at home; as a Black person in Alberta, he is far from home. In this sense, John Ware is exceptional: *he* can belong but his Blackness cannot.

Beyond MacEwan's text, though, the mentions of other Black people in history are frequent enough to cause confusion: how is it that this rich Black history has been almost completely forgotten, or at best, reduced to the singularity of John Ware's story? This misstep in our understanding of the past is partly asserted by common discourse. Often, white people will concede the existence of a "single" Black person or Person of Colour as an exception to the rule that they readily accept: white settlers dominating the land as an unassailable fact. Actually, it's assailable. Even anecdotally I have come across so many accounts of a "single" Black person here or there that it has made me question why people are unwilling to simply put these various incidences together. Don't they see what they add up to?

Because the myth of white predominance prevails, though, most white people don't even think to question the adjacent myth of Black singularity. Indeed, there is a somewhat cynical effect to this assumption: if there is only one Black person – or none at all – recorded in the past, there cannot be any Black history of any substance to note either. After all, one Black cowboy doesn't equal an entire history. Since most Black history in this part of the world has been buried, this leads to the "logical" presumption that John Ware was very probably the only Black person in Alberta while he was alive. Just don't mention his wife. Or his children. Or the people he worked with. Or the people he socialized with. Or the fact that one in four cowboys was Black.[4]

All of these things were facts that I encountered as I dug deep beneath the superficiality of our assumptions. You only have to keep looking. And I kept looking. I'm not a trained historian, but like so many Black people starved of historical legacy, I have had to become my own educator in this regard. I am, however, trained in literary and textual analysis, and those skills are very useful for digging deep, uncovering hidden evidence, separating fact from story. In fact, I felt powerful applying these tools in this context. Words are powerful. Text is powerful. In the case of Black history on the Prairies, text has been used to occlude and exclude Black presence. We have been written over, layer after layer, palimpsestically obscuring our humanity, effectively erasing our complexity, our multi-dimensionality.

For this reason, I have always been interested in recovering examples of Black intellect, thought, and writing. This proves to be a challenging and often painful exercise though. Textual production is largely controlled by white people in our society and this was even more the case in the past. Part of our palimpsestic paving-over involved not having access to the organs of publication. Often, Black communities had to create their own newspaper networks to counter their lack of representation or their misrepresentations in

4 Kenneth W. Porter, "Negro Labor in the Western Cattle Industry, 1866–1900," *Labor History* 10, no. 3 (Summer 1969): 347; David Goldstein-Shirley, "Black Cowboys in the American West: An Historiographical Review," *Ethnic Studies Review* 20 (1997): 79.

mainstream publications. In historical accounts, if we are included at all, it is at the whim of the white author, who usually rendered Black people in simplistic generalities (to suit their own narrative agenda), rarely detailing individual identifiers, often not even providing a name. These factors are compounded by the fact that literacy itself was regularly denied to Black people. Lacking access to reading or writing, it is no wonder that representations of Blackness in historical accounts are as inadequate as they are. Even in the case of *John Ware's Cow Country*, which paints Ware in an unfailingly admirable light, MacEwan still succumbs to this flattening of Black dimensionality. Remember "Sam from Dixie"? Ware is depicted as being surprised at his presence, but this contradicts the readily available facts that MacEwan was surely aware of. There were many Black men in Alberta's early cattle industry, some of whom Ware worked directly with: Billy Welsh, Lige Abel, Pete Smith, and Green Walters to name a few. Typically, "Sam from Dixie" is simply a figure to suit MacEwan's dramatic goals. Sam has a name, but not much else. He has no last name. He has no backstory. He has no ongoing presence in the text. Indeed, after one more brief mention, Sam never shows up again in the rest of the book; like so much of Black history in this part of the world, he has no connection to our present-day, because, unfortunately, he simply has no tomorrow.

Because of this tendency of white authors to ignore our plural backstories and thus evaporate the possibility of our futures, I spend a lot of time trying to identify Black-authored texts that have been overlooked. Moreover, I am prepared to consider forms of authorship that normally defy conventional understanding.

Why not? Convention defied and denied Black textual engagements. I see it as my job to reconnect lost connections. You might even say that history stole humanity from Black people in rendering us textless, and, in making unconventional claims of authorship, I am stealing it back. You only have to keep looking. So, when it came to Black cowboys, not only was it a no-brainer for me to look beyond the singularity of John Ware's presence, but it was natural for me to draw an association between textuality, authorship, and the language of cowboys: cattle brands.

THE SECRET LANGUAGE OF BLACK CATTLE BRANDS

Perhaps the easy association I made between Black literacy and cattle brands is a reflection of my childhood obsession. As a teenager, brand culture seemed a newly-emerged force, but clearly that force had been in play long before the 1980s. We can't forget that our contemporary use of the term in media and marketing is rooted in the original practice of branding cattle. As a teenager, I was already connected to this history and I didn't even know it.

People are quick to point out John Ware was illiterate. But this is only partially true. He appears to have signed some documents himself, and though the initials look shaky, it's almost certainly by his own hand. For one thing, his wife Mildred, who probably did write letters on his behalf (or, at the very least, helped him to write letters), was educated and had a confident stroke.

But I say it is only partially true because in another sense Ware was more than a competent reader, expert even: he read cattle brands. This is an indisputable fact that would have been a necessary skill for a cowboy. It's my feeling that this type of literacy is overlooked because the opposite notion – that he was *illiterate* – satisfies a yearning to understand Ware as a survivor of slavery. It *is* very likely that he was enslaved at some point in his life; the evidence points in that direction. But there is no categorical evidence. He doesn't appear to have said so himself. The vague and curtailed memories his children have of him mentioning his family are attenuated – Nettie once said he never spoke of his family – but they do not directly refer to slavery. If slavery was part of his story, it is clear that he wanted to have nothing more to do with it. How ironic, then, that his storytellers seem obsessed with connecting him to it.

I hardly find this surprising. Many people claim to be progressive and fair-minded when it comes to race, but truly they just mean they don't hate Black people because of the colour of their skin. This doesn't stop them from being susceptible to all manner of narratives that construct and circumscribe People of Colour in myriad ways. I experienced this personally throughout my childhood with basketball and athletics coaches chasing me down in the hallways. They knew nothing about me but my Blackness, and my Blackness was all they needed to know. The story was already filled out from there. The denouement, thrilling; the conclusion, inevitable; the introduction, unnecessary. They read me like a book, but they might as well have been illiterate for all the accuracy their reading rendered.

John Ware, on the other hand, was literate in what we might think of today as a lost language. His own brand is elusive. Variously called "Four Nines" or "Four Walking Sticks" (the latter is more accurate to me), its meaning ignites speculation about — you guessed it — slavery.

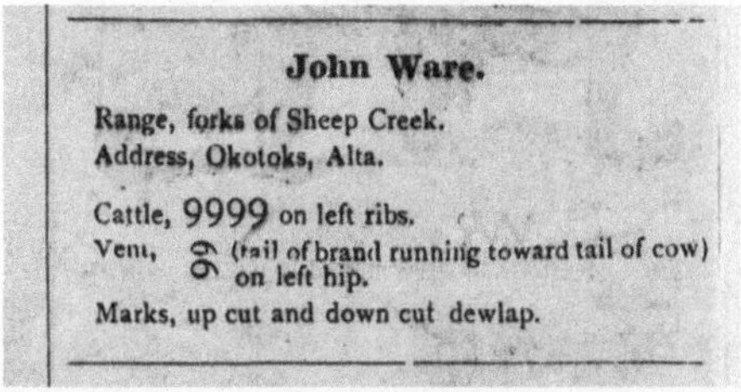

John Ware.

Range, forks of Sheep Creek.
Address, Okotoks, Alta.

Cattle, 9999 on left ribs.
Vent, 9 (tail of brand running toward tail of cow) on left hip.
Marks, up cut and down cut dewlap.

The dominant story is that Ware was nine years old when slavery was abolished and so nine was his "lucky" number. This is almost certainly a story of white people's creation. For someone who spoke so little of his past life, and for whom the evils of slavery — if he did live through them — caused a silence in him as deep and dark as a scar, it doesn't seem likely that he would have memorialized it in a brand. What is more likely, is that they are walking sticks, which is the traditional name of brands that take on that shape. If you peruse historic brand books, you will see that the nine has a shape distinct from the walking stick. The nine is often straighter and has a closed loop. The walking stick is more curved and tends to have a slight opening at the loop. Frustratingly, Ware's brand is something of a hybrid of these styles, but it fits the walking stick much more closely than the number nine.

FIG 1 John Ware's "Four Nines" or "Four Walking Sticks" brand.

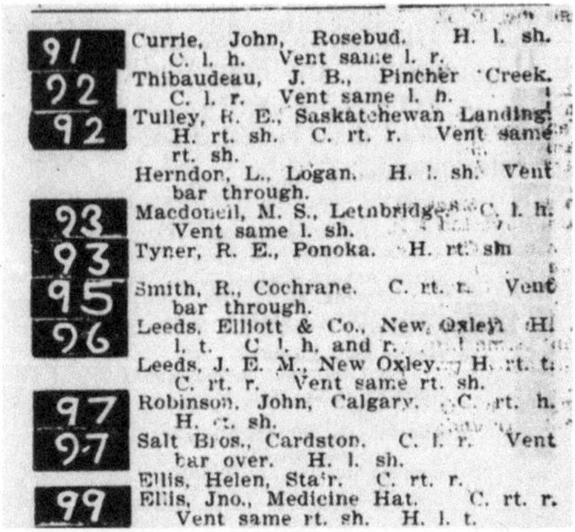

Currie, John, Rosebud. H. l. sh. C. l. h. Vent same l. r.
Thibaudeau, J. B., Pincher Creek. C. l. r. Vent same l. h.
Tulley, R. E., Saskatchewan Landing. H. rt. sh. C. rt. r. Vent same rt. sh.
Herndon, L., Logan. H. l. sh. Vent bar through.
Macdonell, M. S., Lethbridge. C. l. h. Vent same l. sh.
Tyner, R. E., Ponoka. H. rt. sh.
Smith, R., Cochrane. C. rt. r. Vent bar through.
Leeds, Elliott & Co., New Oxley. H. l. t. C. l. h. and r.
Leeds, J. E. M., New Oxley. H. rt. t. C. rt. r. Vent same rt. sh.
Robinson, John, Calgary. C. rt. h. H. rt. sh.
Salt Bros., Cardston. C. l. r. Vent bar over. H. l. sh.
Ellis, Helen, Stair. C. rt. r.
Ellis, Jno., Medicine Hat. C. rt. r. Vent same rt. sh. H. l. t.

There is a code to reading brands that is akin to figurative language. Occasionally it even makes use of figurative language directly. In most cases, it courts certain conceits, certain metaphors. This leaves it open to all manner of interpretations. In this way, again, it is akin to figurative language we might encounter in literature, particularly poetry. It might be said this is what is taking place with John Ware's brand, which is variously read literally (as four nines), symbolically (traditional walking sticks), or figuratively (slavery). Cattle brands can occur as simple letters, as initials, as stylized letters, or as symbols, or they occur as some combination of letters and symbols. They are read in prioritizing order, depending on the particularities of what they visually display. The hard rules for reading brands are as follows: left to right, top to bottom, outside to inside. A famous brand in Alberta, the

FIG 2 Various forms of "9" and "Walking Sticks" and iterations in between.

Bar U brand, is so called because it has a bar floating over top of a capital letter *U*. As there is no left/right or outside/inside to read in this brand, we simply defer to the top/bottom rule, thus: Bar U. If we had placed an *I* after the *U*, the brand would now read Bar UI. If we had moved the *U* above the bar, the brand would read U Bar. And, if we had then added an *I* above that same bar and moved the *U* below, the brand would now read almost as a sentence: I bar you. Some stylizations also encourage phrases and sentence making. Letters with wings are called "flying" brands, while letters perched within an upward turned quarter circle are called "rocking" brands. These sorts of modifications inspire brands that don't give a flying F, compared to other brands that appreciate when things are rocking, eh? These sorts of machinations are endless with brands and contribute to the quality of living language that they can convey.

Here, I'd like to turn to a Black cowboy I mentioned earlier, Green Walters, and discuss his brand. I had mentioned the metaphorizing that is possible with cattle brands and I cautioned against the automatic association between John Ware's brand and its symbolic evocation of slavery. This is because the number nine in and of itself does not evoke any connection to slavery. We, as readers, must force that connection. But with Green Walters, there is a surprisingly strong case that can be made for exactly the interpretation I resent in John Ware's case.

While John Ware was a cowboy's cowboy, Green Walters was something of an interloper. He certainly belonged to the cowboy world, and he eventually managed his own ranch alongside his duties working for others. But he was not a horseman in the same way that Ware was. When it comes to the two key tasks we can clearly assign to cowboying – the roundup and the cattle drive – Walters was an adjacent figure. He participated in these expeditions, but he was often a supporting cast member: cook, wrangler, supply wagon driver. It is clear that he knew the cowboy world and often lived in it; indeed, we must assume that he performed typical cowboy skills when he ran his own ranch – the Gap Ranch – but just as often he found work alongside the conventional cowboy roles.

In this sense he was more of a hustler than typical cowboys because he was prepared to do almost anything to earn a living, not just ride a horse. He is noted in various sources for working as a cook, a hay contractor, a ranch hand, a servant, and a cleaner, among others. I called him a hustler, but more refined Albertans might think of him as a serial entrepreneur. The Gap Ranch, which was located near Billy Cochrane's ranch in the Highwood River valley region in Southern Alberta, was literally a venture to fill in the gaps between gigs with other more established ranchers, like Cochrane's CC Ranch. Walters was well-liked and had an eye for opportunity. But these things were held in an ambivalent tension. He seemed to be a comic figure. J.L. Douglas, a visitor from England, encountered Walters at the Cochrane (or CC) Ranch and called him "very droll," pointing out that "he kept us in roars of laughter all the time."[5] People liked to remark on his body size.

---

5 High River Pioneer and Old Timers' Association, *Leaves from the Medicine Tree* (High River, AB: High River Pioneer and Old Timers' Association, 1960), 307.

Fred Ings, a young ranch hand at the time, said he looked "as broad as he was long."[6] They liked to point out his mannerisms, which they found abrupt and unschooled in a humorous way. They loved to revel in his singing, which they took to reflect the authenticity of his Blackness. In short, they enjoyed having an authentically Black figure of entertainment in their midst.

Perhaps I am being harsh. But I'm sure that Walters saw opportunity in these perceptions of him. In one account, while spending the night at a neighbouring ranch, he is said to have come across boxes of silk pyjamas sent from England that did not fit the owners and so were not used. Aware of the situation, Walters secretly donned layer upon layer until he looked "so round and fat," Fred Ings claimed, "that he was a laughable little figure."[7] When his deception was revealed, he begged clemency, claiming the Englishmen never wore them anyway. Given the tone of the story, it is clear that "the comical little fellow" kept his haul.[8] This is not quite the usual Black "thief" story, but you can see how it courts it, humorously. In yet another account, he is said to have prepared mashed potatoes at the Cochrane Ranch with his fists, pummelling the tubers in a pot, raising the eyebrows of others around him as to the cleanliness of his hands. Mainly, though, his acts are viewed as antics. He was comic relief on the Prairies.

---

6 Frederick William Ings, *Before the Fences: Tales from the Midway Ranch* (Nanton, AB: Nanton Historical Society, 1980), 17.

7 Ings, *Before the Fences*, 18.

8 Ings, *Before the Fences*, 17.

One has to wonder how much this master hustler, who so adeptly shifted from vocation to vocation to make his living, subsisted on the Canadian prairies by ensuring he had a valued place in this society of white people who saw him but didn't quite see him as one of them. Laughter is almost always a balm of appeasement that Black folks have necessarily invoked or performed in the company of white power brokers. It was one more hustle for Walters; it was, if anything, his brand.

But he contained sadness, too. The most striking account of Walters-the-performer is of him singing a spiritual, "Climbing Up the Golden Stairs." We have to recall that this is a period that marked a shift in public perception toward "Negro Spirituals," as they were then called. In the 1880s, when Green Walters arrived in Alberta, the Fisk Jubilee Singers (formed in 1871) had started to carve out a name for themselves and for the legitimacy of spirituals as an art form. Prior to that, these songs were seen as "Negro folk" music, strongly tied to slave plantations. Indeed, they were simply called "slave songs," and so hardly merited anything close to artistic value to the general (white) public. They had been used in entertainment as vehicles for minstrel shows, where the lives of enslaved Africans were caricatured and the horrors of slavery itself minimized for the sake of laughs. We can see, then, how these various accounts of Walters characterize him as reminiscent of minstrel entertainment: from his singing of spirituals to his brutish cooking techniques, he is seen as bombastic, unrefined, hectic, jovial, and disruptive in both comic and tragic ways. Here is how A.E. Cross – who went on to become one of the Big Four who founded the Calgary Stampede — describes Walters singing "Climbing Up the Golden Stairs" to a group of rapt onlookers: "He would start with a low note, gradually getting higher and higher until his emotional feeling would overcome him. With tears streaming down his cheeks he wound up exhausted."[9]

Walters's brand as a performer to white audiences was a reasonable response to his marginalized position in society. But when you consider his cattle brand, you have to conclude he was either a nihilist or a poet. Maybe the two are connected. As with John Ware's brand, there is some mystery as to its inherent symbolism. By this I mean that Ware's brand is recognizable as one of two symbols (nine or walking stick), but it is not clear which one he intended to invoke; similarly, Walter's brand is a recognizable symbol (at least recognizable to his contemporaries) but it was unclear what he intended to invoke with it. Here it might be useful to remind ourselves that the original purpose of cattle brands was to establish distinct ownership. In the early days of the cattle industry, fences were disdained and cattle roamed free to pasture where they wanted for much of the time. Twice during the year, they were gathered together (the process called the "roundup") and inventoried, in fall, to prepare for transport to a cattle market, and in spring, to account for new calves. Because cattle were free to roam wherever they chose, part of the roundup involved separating and sorting cattle with different owners. My brand — B let's

9 Ken Mather, *Frontier Cowboys and the Great Divide: Early Ranching in B.C. and Alberta* (Surrey, BC: Heritage House, 2013), 169.

say — would be burned into the hide of all my cattle, so that when it came for the sorting, I could separate out and claim the ones with my *B* visibly on some part of their torso. Equally, if any one of the cows with my *B* emblazoned on their side was milking calves, I could reasonably claim the calves as well.

So, at bottom, branding was about ownership. And what more fraught system of ownership existed in Walters's lifetime than that of slavery? It was a system that abrogated freedom, stripped humanity from human beings, and conferred the category of chattel, all of which were understood as inheritable traits. There is no conclusive evidence about it, but, as with John Ware, it is very likely that Green Walters was enslaved at some point in his life. Though he had enormous talents, he was what economists today would call "unskilled." This is corroborated by his transient life and his many and restless labour roles. I called him a hustler, yes, because he was forced to find whatever means he could to make a living — because he had very likely been deprived of any education or vocational training that could have assured him a profession in life. On censuses, he is regularly noted as lacking literacy. He also consistently indicates he was born in Missouri, which was a slave state, and his parents were born in Kentucky, also a slave state. In fact, many proponents of slavery moved from Kentucky (and other slave states) to establish plantations in northern Missouri, along the Missouri River as part of westward expansion. The region was colloquially known as Little Dixie, acknowledging the culture of the planters who settled there from the 1820s to the 1850s. So the geographic trajectory fits the timeline of Walters's family story.

The glaring piece of evidence, however, is the fact that he is only present in American census records *after* the Civil War. Other than to count them, and perhaps note their gender and age, enslaved Africans were almost never mentioned in censuses. (In fact, most of this accounting was done in official Slave Schedules, which were distinct from the formal censuses you're familiar with.) This lacuna in the historical record is a blotch that also appends itself to the living life of Blackness on this continent, and so, too, it has appended itself to Green Walters.

His ascendancy, then, within the cattle industry, from itinerant labourer to ranch owner is a triumph. Yes, it was a "small" ranch, we are repeatedly told in the records, but this should not take away from the achievement. Green Walters was an owner. And here his brand courts a puzzling if not powerful meaning. Also called Ox Yoke, the Double Yoke brand was a familiar symbol to cattle folk and agrarians alike. The curved humps represented the bows in the wooden yokes fastened to oxen's necks for them to pull ploughs or other implements. The symbolism of such shackling was not lost on anyone, and during Walters's lifetime it was common to refer to the "yoke" of slavery. The language is seeded deep in our social consciousness: it shows up in the Bible in Ephesians 26, and like so much of Christian religious tradition, it was taken up and adapted by enslaved Africans in the Americas. Frederick Douglass, the most celebrated and influential abolitionist of the nineteenth century, regularly invoked the "yoke of slavery" in his talks. Formerly enslaved himself, his trajectory represents a success along the lines of Walters's, though to considerably wider public effect.

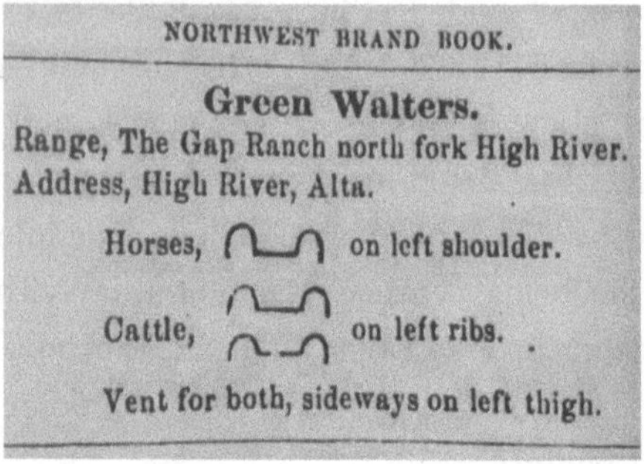

NORTHWEST BRAND BOOK.

Green Walters.

Range, The Gap Ranch north fork High River.
Address, High River, Alta.

Horses, on left shoulder.

Cattle, on left ribs.

Vent for both, sideways on left thigh.

My point is, in Walters's lifetime, the association between an ox yoke and slavery would have been a given for Black people. What then to make of his cattle brand? I choose to think of it as poetry. If the figuring capacity of brands has in the past invited white people to understand Ware's brand as a sign in relation to his victimhood – that is, as an object of slavery whose "lucky" number can only reflect either bondage or freedom as states imposed on him beyond his control – then I can choose to understand Walters's brand as an assertion of his agency, his control, *his* state of ownership within a social and economic system whose capital, potentially, used to assert him as owned. This is an entirely different kind of figurative play; he remains attached to the symbolizing of slavery that appears to have permanently associated itself with Blackness on this continent, but he has reconfigured the association; he has doubled down on its meaning and thus doubled its meaning; he has re-metaphorized what it means to be yoked. This is his poetry, his personal brand, his Double Yoke.

FIG 3 "Double Yoke."

You may say that all of this speculation is purely subjective on my part, that I am forcing my meanings. I don't deny this. I simply suggest another way of looking at it: I am not forcing meaning; I am stealing it. And I do so out of the historical legacy of Blackness that I can claim in a doubled way, like Green Walters: I claim the category of thief that was imposed on me, on my Blackness, *and* I claim the process of thievery that I inherited through my family's historical legacy.

Long before I ever knew about Black cowboys on the Prairies, or their metaphorizing powers with branding irons, I was a confused teenager shoplifting my way into a stereotype. Somehow, I felt powerful doing so, even though I also felt trapped at the same time. One source of confusion for me had to do with my dubious sense of belonging. To this day, I am not convinced that I am justified in claiming the history of Black cowboys (I do so despite the doubt), nor was I convinced as a teenager that I could claim the authenticity of my African identity. Growing up, I certainly felt Canadian, particularly Albertan, but that sense of belonging was regularly challenged by other Canadians, other Albertans, who clearly did *not* see me in this way. This was confusing to me, but despite my thoroughly Canadian experiences, my upbringing was actually hybrid.

At school and out in public, I lived an ordinary Canadian life, racism notwithstanding. When I stepped inside my home, though, things changed. For much of my childhood, my home was African.

The longer my parents lived here, the more our household morphed into something more recognizably Canadian, but during my early years my parents' African sensibilities dominated. We ate African food, spoke an African language, played African music, and regularly visited with the wider Afro-Caribbean community, such as it existed in Edmonton and Calgary in the seventies and eighties. The experience was distinct enough that I would occasionally feel things were amiss at my friends' homes when, for example, people would just sit around the table, quietly speaking, or sit in the living room merely talking, until it was time to go, and rarely did anyone even suggest turning on music, let alone bust out onto the dance floor to celebrate the miracle of rhythm.

At the same time, however, I struggled to see our version of African culture as authentically African at all. Our "African" foods were laced with bizarre delicacies. One of our signature "ethnic" foods was a salad called "Salon Salad." This concoction featured oddities mixed together like baked beans and canned salmon. Once in a while this had me raising an eyebrow. Baked beans? How is that African? There were other "traditional" foods that baffled me, like tinned sardines, roast beef, and marmalade sandwiches. Weren't these foods I also regularly saw in the kitchens of my white friends?

Occasionally, I would also question my parents' musical choices. When my mother talked about the music she loved when she was young, she rhapsodized about the Beatles and The Byrds. My dad favoured barbershop quartets, swooping his bass notes in chorus with Mitch Miller and the Gang. A family favourite was the soundtracks of popular musicals: *My Fair Lady*, *West Side Story*, and above all *Fiddler on the Roof*. Even at the jubilant parties they threw, the most popular songs were often reggae and African remakes of pop hits. Blondie's "The Tide is High" reigned for one part of the eighties. Paul Simon's "Graceland" dominated the next.

While these anomalies disturbed my sense of Africanness somewhere deep beneath the surface of my identity, nothing caused me more struggle than Krio, the Sierra Leonean language we spoke. Whereas my friends would blink in bafflement at what struck them as an utterly foreign language, Krio just sounded like a version of English to me. This was not just my sense of fluency, having been immersed in both English and Krio from infancy; rather, Krio is a creole language that incorporates elements of French, Portuguese, and English. The history of Sierra Leone is such that this mixture is inevitable. The base of Krio *is* English, but the grammar follows African rules, and many African words have been co-opted from neighbouring ethnic groups, such as Mende and Temne, as well as from other West African countries, like Ghanaian Akan and Nigerian Yoruba.

But all my self-conscious teenage ears could attune themselves to was the English structure that held Krio up. When wide-eyed white kids would ask me to produce a magic word in this other language, the existence of which fascinated their imaginations, I would try to identify the least English-sounding word I could. But it always felt false to me, inauthentic. "Well," I remember saying to a girl I was trying to impress in eighth grade, "how about *mɛk ɛs*? It means *hurry up* or *get a move on*." This did produce exactly the kind of awe-struck validation I was hoping for, but it also produced a sense of duplicity in me, a feigning toward Africa that I did not feel justified to claim. To my ears, *mɛk ɛs* simply sounded like "make haste," which was just English. Worse, it was English mispronounced, English poorly pronounced by African mouths who had stolen someone else's language and were trying to pass it off as their own. Recall my struggle with my Uncle Biola pronouncing my name as "Bat." All of this simply reinforced those struggles. Even my family name, *Bickersteth*, is European and not an indigenous African name![10]

How did this travesty come to be? An entire cultural group stealing someone else's culture? How was it, I wondered to myself, that I came from a people who had institutionalized thievery to the point of seeing it as a legitimate form of their own identity? How could I possibly call myself African when much of what I understood of my African background seemed to rely so heavily on European – specifically English – cultural references? With this sense of Krio being a stealing culture of stolen artifacts, it is no wonder that I did not feel I could authentically claim my African background as something to root me in a tradition that properly accounted for the clear "non-Canadianness" that white Canadians regularly saw in me.

In fact, I had it backwards. I had accepted the stereotype of Black thief because it gave me an ambivalent sense of power; it was one of the defining identities I was permitted by the dominant

---

10 Although the word "indigenous" is normally capitalized when discussing the communities associated with Turtle Island, for the most part I will refrain from using this capitalization when discussing other contexts of indigeneity.

white culture to inhabit. But once you understand yourself in a certain light, you begin to understand everything else in that same way. I was a thief; therefore, in my mind, I was descended from a culture of thieves. It never occurred to me, though, that I saw things in this way because society had already yoked me to them. I didn't know it then, but the thing that would eventually rescue my perspective, and so rescue me from this particular metaphorizing, was a kind of doubling down that I now recognize as Green Walters's Double Yoke.

The history of Sierra Leone is complex and intertwined with the West through what George Elliott Clarke calls the "crucible of the slave trade."[11] This may surprise you, but remember, this is how history works: the more you delve past the surface, the more you encounter the essence of *that thing* deep down that barely bleeds to the surface. When you study slavery, it boggles the mind at how far-reaching and deeply integrated it is with the formation of the modern West and, thus, the alteration of so many peoples and cultures around the world. The key geographical relationship is demonstrated as a triangle between Africa, the Americas, and Europe. This is sometimes known as the triangular trade: Europeans travelled down to Africa, acquired slaves, shipped them to the Americas, and then transferred the wealth they amassed from free, enforced labour back to Europe. At one point during

11 George Elliott Clarke, "Must All Blackness Be American?: Locating Canada in Borden's Tightrope Time, or Nationalizing Gilroy's The Black Atlantic," in *Odysseys Home: Mapping African-Canadian Literature* (Toronto: University of Toronto Press, 2002), 73.

this torrid history, Africans who had been enslaved in the U.S. found themselves in Canada, freed from slavery's tyranny, as a result of supporting the British cause against the newly formed Americans during the Revolutionary War, 1775–83. It should be pointed out that these Black Loyalists, as they are known, established Canada's longest-standing populations of Black communities in Canada. Two hundred and fifty years later, their descendants thrive in Nova Scotia today. At the time, though, these early Black Canadians found that slavery was only ambivalently present in Canada; some regions ignored it, some didn't. Some parts enforced it, others didn't. That meant there were actual, enslaved Africans on Canadian soil at the same time that these Black Loyalists arrived. Rather than realize the full scope of their anticipated freedom, they entered a territory of confusion. Many European settlers still saw them as people who may, perhaps, be free, but whose Blackness was the mark of their enduring capacity to be enslaved. Effectively, they were viewed as inferior people, even subhuman. As such, they struggled for equal opportunities (the farmland that had been promised to them, for example, was either inadequate or never materialized), and eventually, out of utter frustration, demanded to be returned to Africa. Without providing every detail of this complex history, their request was eventually granted and in 1792 about 1,200 of them sailed in a flotilla of freedom back to Africa, where they founded their capital: Freetown.

I want to pause here because this is a moment of history's poetry: the impossible return. Sometimes, we think of figurative language or cultural moments as providing a "turn." And here, we have the culmination of a "turn" in its repetition, the turn and the return. The African stolen from home now turns back to home. But poetry's beauty is nothing if not backstabbing. Accomplishing the impossible return after crossing the dreaded Atlantic through the Door of No Return – being turned into objects of labour, etc., only to reclaim that which had been irretrievably lost – is an accomplishment of triumph. But it is also impossible. When one turns, and turns again, one cannot turn one's back on what was left behind. Indeed, the Africans who remained permanently displaced in the Americas have proven this over time, imbuing so much of American culture with sensibilities that were retained across the Atlantic. Similarly, the Nova Scotians who turned back to Africa could not fully turn their backs on Canada, the U.S., or the West in general.

In fact, the project to relocate them to Africa was itself supported by European financial backers whose argument was that this new colony in Africa would be a beacon of Western achievement on the continent; it would demonstrate to the world that Africans could fashion functioning societies embedded with Western principles; it would prove that Africans could be civilized. This was an experiment to rival the democratic experiment that had also very recently birthed the United States of America. The two are intertwined. So it was that these newest Africans would have a European education, would worship a European God, would dress like Europeans, would hold European values, would speak a European language. Over time, though, African sensibilities would also infiltrate their culture, and this mixture came to define them. Somewhat pejoratively, they were known as Afro-Saxons. They were understood to be a creolized culture.[12] Their very name, *Krio*, was thought to be a creolized derivation of the word *Creole* itself. (This turns out not to be true; Krio is actually derived from a Yoruba term, *Akiriyo*, which was a reference to our tendency to walk about regularly, specifically going to church often.[13])

We had been stamped with the marks of so many different layers of culture and history that we appeared to have no original stamp of our own. We were a maverick culture. This maverick nature *is* to some extent our brand, not in the sense of being rebellious, but in the sense of being distinct for lacking a mark.[14] There is something deeply appropriate about having the brand of absence. In a sense, it is how one encounters Blackness over and over again in the dominant perspectives of historical accounts,

---

12 I should point out that two more elements of hybridization occurred. Jamaican Maroons, who had been relocated to Nova Scotia in their convoluted historical path for freedom, were eventually settled in Freetown in 1800. Also, throughout much of the nineteenth century, the British Navy patrolled the coast of West Africa in an effort to put an end to slavery (this impulse resulted from another convoluted historical path that is beyond the scope of my text). They intercepted slave ships, arrested the slavers, and returned the captured Africans to Freetown, regardless of whatever part of Africa they were taken from originally. These two factors, the Maroons and the returned captives, injected more layers of mixture into the Krio character.

13 Clifford N. Fyle and Eldred D. Jones, *A Krio–English Dictionary* (Oxford: Oxford University Press and Sierra Leone University Press, 1980), 203.

14 This is the original sense of the term: Samuel Augustus Maverick was a Texas rancher known for neglecting to brand his calves. Stray calves, roaming unbranded, became known as "mavericks."

particularly Western Canadian historical accounts: unremarked, ciphers, absent. When I was young, I had no knowledge of any Black history on the Prairies at all. I also had only the barest understanding of Sierra Leone's history. I had no idea, for example, that this West African nation that my family was from literally shared history with Canada. To this day, most Canadians have little or no knowledge of the historical links between Sierra Leone and Nova Scotia. But it was like that for everything having to do with Black humanity. The notion of Blackness was presented as opaque and ahistoric. (Now you know why so many people do a double-take when they learn that Egypt is in the Middle East *and* Africa: Africa is a black amorphous lump of no-history. Egypt is historical and not Black. How could it be in Africa?) It is no surprise that I didn't even search out Black history on the Prairies, nor that I saw the essence of my African identity – of the Krio people in general – as fraudulent, as empty of history, when in fact it was the complete opposite: the Krio are authentically who we are *because* of history. On top of that, as I later discovered, Alberta and the Canadian Prairies are rich with Black history. When you scratch the surface, you don't find a paucity, you rupture opacity; you find a Prairie Blackness that is rife with history.

Here is where my concern with Black history on the Prairies and the history of the Krio of Sierra Leone created surprising and fruitful parallels for me. The nothingness of Black history – that is, the perception that Blackness lacks history – allowed me as a teenager to find a comforting power in becoming a thief, a stereotype. Stereotypes, of course, have no history; they only have story, which is a powerful force that influences us as much as the physical forces of the universe (often more so). And different people see different things in the same story. For me, thievery was access to power because it gave me visibility. All of my life I struggled to be seen in a society that was largely blind to the multi-dimensionality of my humanity. Succumbing to a stereotype of Blackness seemed to solve one side of the equation for me (being seen), even if it problematized the other (being seen as human). This self-perception also conveniently explained my Africanness to me: the Krio stole their culture from others. When you see yourself in a certain light, it is inevitable that you shine that same light on others as well. Slave holders did not originally fear Black revolt and Black violence against them because they saw Blackness as inherently violent, but because they recognized their own enacted violence on innocent people being reflected back at them (thus shaping the *story* that Blackness was inherently violent). Even Thomas Jefferson who apparently supported some form of freedom for enslaved Africans, could not bring himself to be an out and out abolitionist. He, too, feared a violent uprising. Nobody bothered to ask the enslaved people themselves. This is how the light you shine on yourself becomes the light you shine on others. You displace your own faults onto another.

One of the Black cowboys I have encountered while scratching the surface is Thomas Rife. Rife lived in Southern Alberta at the beginning of the twentieth century and pops up a handful of times in local newspapers. Here is one of the contexts in which I discovered him:

FOUR PRISONERS

SENTENCED AT CALGARY

Chief Justice Sifton Imposes Heavy Sentences. Three Years for horse Stealing

Bulletin Special Dispatch.

Calgary, August 3.—Chief Justice Sifton had four prisoners arraigned today. All pleaded guilty and were sentenced as follows:

Michael Bodner, three years at Stony Mountain for stabbing a miner named Ruly at Canmore.

Samuel Bruneau, three years for horse stealing.

John Percy, one year in Regina jail for stealing from the Hudson's Bay store.

Thomas Rife, one year for obtaining board under false pretences.

At this point, I didn't know I had stumbled across a Black cowboy. Unusually for the time, no mention of Rife's race is made. This is particularly unusual given the criminal context that exists. I may have guessed that Rife was somehow related to the cattle world, at least distantly, because he was involved in an incident of horse-stealing. But that would have been a speculative conclusion. What is clear from the article is that Rife's role in the caper involved a form of fraudulence: "Thomas Rife [sentenced] one year for obtaining board under false pretences." Later, when I found

FIG 4 Discovering Thomas Rife.

references to him being a "negro cow puncher," I realized I had accidentally discovered another Black cowboy. This is one of the ways in which the rhymes of history hurt. I had identified another forgotten cowboy, but the context was once again criminality, fraudulence. The power of this trope — the thieving Black *blank* — was demonstrated in its longevity. The consistency of its essence over such a long period of time only reaffirmed its ahistoricity. It's no wonder it held an appeal for me as a teenager. That power seemed to say that history doesn't matter; dimensionality is irrelevant: you can be immortal. Yes, the Prairies are rife with Black history, but Black history seems rife with Thomas Rifes.

My Krio history also felt rife with Rifes. Fraudulence seemed everywhere, but nowhere more to me than in the language. Yet it was this collision of rife and Rife that helped to show me another understanding beyond the inevitable thievery. As I pointed out earlier, Krio words, like *mɛk ɛs*, just sounded like broken English to me. But, truly, because of how taken I was with understanding myself through the lens of a thief, I was missing the point about how the language works and the inherent poetry it can express. For example, I heard the word *Krio* as a lazy version of *Creole* with the *l* sound dropped and the pronunciation altered. *Beans* became ornamented in Krio with *ch* at the end, making it *binch*. And, occasionally, there is the insertion of an Africanization. One of the ways of saying, "I will be [right] back," is *A de kam*, where *de* is a wholly new substitute for "will be" or, more accurately in this case, "am." In fact, linguists say that this use of *de* reflects substrate language structures (West African grammatical rules) more so than superstrate (English/colonial) ones.[15] The literal translation of *A de kam* is "I am coming," but this is a very limited translation and does not at all do justice to the language. For instance, this same sentence can also be used as a statement of departure. In other words, you say it not when you are coming, but when you are leaving. Krio is not the only version of a West African "pidgin" to construct the connotation in this way, but in the case of Krio it is certainly poetic.

It could be said that British involvement in the African slave trade began in Sierra Leone. John Hawkins, a British trader, is one of the first people to sail from England to collect Africans and transport them across the Atlantic to the Americas and transform their lives and multiple continents forever. Hawkins, then, is the first thief on my complicated, implicating family tree. He made three initial visits to what was then known as the Guinea Coast of Africa between 1562 and 1568. On his first trip, he captured roughly 400 Africans along the Sierra Leone river and took them to Hispaniola in the Caribbean, where he made an enormous profit.[16] This lucrative introduction kicked off England's involvement in the transatlantic slave trade.[17] Two centuries later, the famous hymn "Amazing Grace" was written by John Newton who had

---

15 Malcolm Awadajin Finney, "Substratal Influence on the Morphosyntactic Properties of Krio," *Linguistic Discovery* 2, no. 2 (2004): 66.

16 Zubairu Wai, *Epistemologies of African Conflicts: Violence, Evolutionism, and the War in Sierra Leone* (New York: Palgrave Macmillan, 2012), 60.

17 Fun fact: On his third voyage to Sierra Leone, Hawkins was joined by Sir Francis Drake, a controversial national hero of England.

worked on a slave ship as a sailor and also sailed to Sierra Leone to collect slaves. The venture that Hawkins had initiated was now a full-fledged institution. “I once was blind, but now can see” was meant to express Newton’s transformation into a Christian as well as an abolitionist. He didn’t, though, completely extricate himself from the fiendish industry immediately after his conversion, so powerful was its economic pull. From the African perspective, the Atlantic slave trade was a kind of death (often it was literally so). Family members, friends, and loved ones who were taken were never seen again, except in very rare cases. Very much like death, return was impossible.

Except when it wasn’t. When 1,200 disgruntled Black people left Nova Scotia for Sierra Leone, they managed the impossible. For some, it was metaphorical; they had been born in the Americas and were bridging generational displacement in re-establishing themselves in Africa. For a small few, it was literal: they had been stolen from Africa in their youth, and years later found themselves returning to their lost home. For everyone, it was an extraordinary feat of reasserting historical agency. What had begun, roughly in 1562–63 with John Hawkins’s first voyage, had finally culminated in 1792 when the first of the Nova Scotian flotilla touched land. The impossible return through the curtain of death. Why *shouldn’t* they have flipped their language? Why *wouldn’t* such a poetic legacy express itself in inversions? This simple saying doesn’t allow for departure: *A de kam*, even when one is leaving, always speaks of the promise of coming. In this way, the people who became the impossible returners, always orient themselves toward home.

This simple poetry of history entirely escaped me in my youth. I could not see this advancement on the European language that had been historically imposed on us. It seemed only to be a broken or substandard version of it to me. I could not hear the history rife with poetry in Krio. It is only now, as an adult, that I can accept that maybe we were thieves of a sort because thieving was forced on us. Because we were stolen, we had English forced on us. And, maybe, because we had English forced on us, we stole English. And then, even more poetically, maybe in stealing it, we returned to it and, in so doing, returned it to poetry. Maybe some ancestor of mine had Bickersteth forced on them. Maybe they stole Bickersteth. Maybe in stealing it, they returned us to it.

Thomas Rife had "thief" forced on him. Maybe he was a thief. Maybe, like me as a teenager, he claimed a difficult poetry, and in so doing carved out a contradictory agency: maybe he *chose* to be the thief he was expected to be. Maybe he found the impossible return to his humanity. I don't know. There are very few historical records regarding his life. But he's not an absence. He made sure of that. Even if he died in a prison in Selkirk, Manitoba.[18]

---

18 I don't know for certain that he died in prison. I just know, like so much of Black history, his documented life delivers nothing more.

PART 3

MARKS OF THE BEAST

INTERMEZZO

In the summer of 2025, I started to sketch out an idea for an opera. Opera is not one of my go-to genres but recently it has started to appeal to me. Earlier that year I had been invited by the Calgary Philharmonic Chorus to give a talk on the unrecorded development of jazz on the Prairies, featuring Clarence Washington, a completely unknown Black pianist who played live music in cinemas in Central Alberta. After the talk, one of the members pointed out how operatic Washington's life seemed. He suggested I consider writing a libretto dramatizing his story. "After all," he suggested, "you are a writer and your sister is an opera singer." Inwardly, I blinked. I don't know why I had never made that association before. My sister *is* a trained opera singer, though she has had to pivot in strategic ways to cobble a life for herself in the arts. The operatic world has only very recently started reconsidering its stranglehold on European priorities, so, in the meantime, while opera was trying to figure out how to "do better," she had to earn a living. She's still a singer, and she still sings opera, but she has added several other skill sets (theatre, dance, film, choral, etc.) to her repertoire.

I think my direct connection to opera didn't occur to me, in part, because Neema's trajectory did not land her in the centre of the genre's world. Another part of it, though, is that I have not really been drawn to opera in my life, though I am a music lover and come from a family of music lovers. The closest I got to it is with my parents' fondness for *Fiddler on the Roof*, and musicals are only (barely) opera-adjacent. Opera has simply never strongly appealed to me.

Perhaps, that has even influenced the classical composers I prefer, Beethoven (1 opera), Brahms (0 operas), Mahler (half an opera, if reworking someone else's counts). The real challenge for me, though, is exactly what Neema experienced, that most operas take on themes and explore narratives that quite thoroughly erase us.

But the genre is still very compelling to me. It is bombastic and dramatic and collides music, dance, theatre on a large scale; it produces its magic by overloading the senses, and very often the theme of a particular opera involves someone being overwhelmed or something being overwhelming. That cornucopia of possibility seems very appropriate to exploring various Black histories, particularly those that court tumult. A couple days after delivering my talk to the Philharmonic Chorus, I sketched out a basic plot for a libretto on Clarence Washington's life. And then, in the way these things often happen, as I was imagining a dramatic arc for Clarence Washington, I kept jotting down notes for an entirely different story with a completely different set of characters.

This new story's working title was "Jealous Guy," and had the most innocuous plotline: Jimmy and Charlie are brothers who have fallen out, and Rupe, the brothers' cousin, has replaced Jimmy as Charlie's BFF. Jimmy, a wildly imaginative, scheming brainiac, blames the rift on the failure of their last business venture. He is convinced his next business idea will fix everything and make them millions. All he needs is a royal army, an empty country, and ten thousand African slaves. No problem, right? Oh, sorry: didn't I say? The year is 1670, and Jimmy's brother, Charlie? He's the King of England.

The opera charts the birth of the Hudson's Bay Company, which rose out of the financial ashes of the RAC, the Royal African Company, a business that traded in slaves. This relationship between the Hudson's Bay Company and the Royal African Company has hardly been explored but it is central to sweeping transformations that disparately impacted three continents and their Indigenous inhabitants, contributed to the invention of modernity, and paved the way for the geopolitical and economic structures that currently dominate the globe.[19] We are so focused on slavery as an American institution that we forget it was a global phenomenon with the participation of numerous countries, as well as financial systems that were deeply integrated and implicated with each other. Beyond the Underground Railroad, most Canadians struggle to see *any* connections between slavery and Canada. The truth is, although there are certainly a number of steps in between, frankly, you might say that it was the idea of slavery that eventually begat the idea of Canada. What an opera, right? (COC, go right ahead and commission me; I'll wait.)

One of the things that appeals to me in telling this story is the opportunity to flip historical relationships inside out, making the invisible visible and forcing us to reckon with something that deeply problematizes how we understand ourselves to be who we

---

19 I actually came across an account of this connection in much greater detail earlier this year in Niigaan Sinclair's *Wînipêk: Visions of Canada from an Indigenous Centre* (Toronto: McLelland & Stewart, 2025). Shout out to my Indigenous brothers and sisters who keep advancing the work of centring historical frameworks that have been conveniently ignored in the past. ✊🏿

are. It's one of my signature moves. The simplest example of this is my exploration of Black cowboys. We can no longer understand the social landscape of the West in the same way when we acknowledge that its composition has been historically different from what we've been led to believe. For some people, this is a discomforting challenge that they struggle to accept. For others, it is a welcome surprise that opens new possibilities of understanding for them. I recognize and want to acknowledge both experiences. Discovering and identifying Black cattle brands is reconciling and empowering, and it makes me feel closer than most other ways to a valid "Albertanness" that usually eludes me. At the same time, there is a dark side to this history that also makes me feel discomfort and challenged in unexpected ways. And, if my expectation is for others to confront their sense of discomfort when I reveal these hidden histories, then I, too, must confront my own discomfort as directly and honestly as possible.

HBC'S SECRET SKIN

One of the tools of dramatic power that I envision for "Jealous Guy" is that the identities of the two principal characters are not made obvious right away. Jimmy doesn't make us think of James, the future King James II of England. This is because namings are powerful. The namer has power. Before James became King of England, he was Duke of York. And it is as the Duke of York that he established the RAC with his brother Charles. In some ways, I like this story because it appeals to a side of me – maybe Albertan – that enjoys innovation, even entrepreneurial innovation, particularly the inventiveness of it. I sometimes liken it to artistic creativity. But mainly, this story horrifies me. And this horror appeals to another side of me – certainly writerly – that is fascinated with inhumanity as a dramatic expression of humanity. Prince Andrew, the current Duke of York, is not the same Duke of York from the late 1600s. But the continuity of the name demonstrates a persistence in the legacy of wealth and power of the royal family.[20]

We are all very good at naming things in ways that erase what we don't want to see and reinforce what we want to get. The convenient retooling of the Hudson's Bay Company first to The Bay, and then to the acronym, HBC, has gracefully elided the territorial appetite of the colonialism that impelled it. Who would bother to think about the displacement of Indigenous people or the spreading of smallpox when you are buying a pair of socks on a credit card marked HBC? What could those three letters possibly have to do with that? Equally, who would think that slavery has anything to do with HBC?

But it does. There are three key ways in which the two are connected. First and most importantly, they were connected through money. The first royal venture in slave trading was not entirely

20 Within a few months of writing this section, the ongoing scandal of Andrew's involvement in Brian Epstein's sex trafficking ring culminated in his removal from official duties and the stripping of his royal titles. It is a startlingly rare example of a reckoning for the very rich and powerful. Rightly, this particular Duke of York is no more. But the Dukedom of York may yet continue.

successful. The Company of Royal Adventurers Trading into Africa was established with a royal charter in 1660 but suffered from a number of financial setbacks for over a decade, including an intense war from 1665–67 with the Dutch (who were competitors in West Africa), the outbreak of the Great Plague of London (1665) and the devastation it brought, and the Great Fire of London (1666) and the further decimation it caused. It was not a great decade for startups. Eventually, the company folded in 1672, but not before it had established a key network of funders among London's wealthy, among them King Charles II, his brother James, the Duke York, and their cousin, Prince Rupert of the Rhine. These people provided the initial capital for the Hudson's Bay Company in 1670 on the basis of their previous financial relationship with the African ventures. Another key connection is in the template of monopoly the African trade offered. The royal charters established monopolies for the Crown, clearing the way for its dominance in the slave trade. Monopolies were enforced as legal entities whose structures were then copied into the HBC charter. The third key connection is the concept of sovereign dominance. This, too, was copied into the HBC charter. The concept encouraged the Crown to privatize and administer large swaths of land in the manner of a sovereign nation. In the mind of the Crown, it justified taking control of much of West Africa because it was an ungoverned, wild territory. The establishment of Prince Rupert's Land on this continent is the direct result of this concept. Most Canadians are under the false assumption that the heinous acts of slavery have little or nothing to do with Canada at all. But as you can see, the connections between the HBC and slavery are deeply interwoven and deeply integrated through legal structures, concepts of sovereignty, and networks of financial support.

Now let's confront a particularly heinous practice of slavery that the very same Duke of York who helped to conceive the Hudson's Bay Company engaged in. It is a practice that raises questions for my project of recognizing forms of Black agency in common, everyday ranching practices on the Canadian Prairies. Here is a quote from Elizabeth Donnan's compilation of slave trading documents, this one describing a slave castle on the coast of present-day Ghana:

> In the area of this Quadrangle . . . are large Vaults, with an iron Grate at the Surface to let in Light and Air on those poor Wretches, the Slaves, who are chained and confined there till a Demand comes. They are all marked with a burning Iron upon the right Breast, D.Y. Duke of York.[21]

The English monarchy's involvement in, and consequential wealth from, acquiring and selling enslaved Africans was pervasive and far-reaching. What had begun with John Hawkins's three speculative journeys in the 1560s saw little development until the formation of the Royal African Company a century later. After an inconsistent decade of mostly losing money, the company hit

---

21 Elizabeth Donnan, ed., *Documents Illustrative of the History of the Slave Trade to America*, vol. 2, *The Eighteenth Century* (Washington, D.C.: Carnegie Institution of Washington, 1931), 269.

its stride and launched England into the stratosphere of wealth generators. England cultivated the most lucrative trade in slaves out of all the other European countries. This carried on throughout the Stuart monarchy's reign. James was the original director of the company. His brand, the DY brand, is referred to often in contemporaneous documents, but no surviving image of it exists. However, a later brand, used by the South Sea Company (which was sponsored by Queen Anne) has survived. This brand is tangible evidence of the monarchy's involvement and shows that involvement to be multigenerational.

FIG 5 "Mark for Negroes": South Sea Company Brand. From the British Library Collection: Additional Manuscripts 2557, fo18r.

The brand was only recently discovered (reported in 2023) in a document discussing an agreement between the monarchs of England and Spain.[22] Queen Anne, the last Stuart monarch of England, and King Phillip of Spain had already established an agreement (an *assiento*) for trading slaves in the Spanish territories of the Caribbean. This document was a directive to specifically use the brand for the South Sea Company as the official brand for these purposes.

> Know ye, that we the Royal Assiento Company for Negros and appointed Pursuant to the Contract between her Late Britannick Majesty Queen Anne (now in Glory) and His Catholick Majesty: Phillip 5th, do hereby Certify and Declare that the mark henceforward to be put upon the Bodys of the Negros to be Sold and Dispos'd of in the Spanish West Indies, for and on the Account of this Comp. and of the said assiento, is and shall be according to the Mark in the Margin of this Instrument being the Usuall Mark of this Company In Witness whereof we have caused our Common Seal to be Hereunto affixed Dated the Eighth Day of March Anno Domini 1714 and in the first year of King George.[23]

---

22 Karla Adam, "A Crown Branded onto Bodies Links British Monarchy to Slave Trade," *Washington Post*, 28 September 2023, https://www.washingtonpost.com/world/2023/09/28/slave-trade-monarchy-uk-archives/

23 Adam, "A Crown Branded onto Bodies."

My fascinated horror splits into two paths: first, I am intrigued by the design. I can't help thinking that it is clever in the manner of visual symbols that instantly render their meaning in a unique way. Although stylized symbols of this type don't have clear-cut names, in the language of cattle brands we might call this brand "crown over connected S reverse-C C reverse-S." I can't help myself; I find it clever. Brands of this type are no longer in use because all of their intricacies are so easily lost when transferred to the cattle's hide, quickly becoming blotches over time. Fittingly, these stylized brands are known as "Spanish" brands because they were largely used in the earliest phase of cattle branding in North America, and it was Spanish *vaqueros* who began the tradition here. The other path my split brain takes has precisely to do with the brand's intricate design. I can't help but think how many lines of hot iron it represents. All that intricacy, translating into a complex of agony against the skin. How callous, to come up with such a mark whose design so carelessly multiplies pain. This is the exuberance of a burgeoning rococo style, rendering its excess in self-indulgence, an excess that ultimately negates the humanity of each African's chest it pressed itself to.

Of course, my musings are absurd. *All* brand designs were a callous dismissal of our humanity, from curlicued serifed letters to straightlaced single bars. How ironic it was for me to then come across instructions for caring for the stricken flesh of the branded. These are directed to the captain of the Dutch slave ship *De Nieuwe Hoop*, but were regulations generally expected of the Dutch West India Company during the seventeenth century.

> As you purchase slaves you must mark them at the upper right arm with the silver marker cc n, which is sent along with you for that purpose. Note the following when you do the branding: (1) The area of marking must first be rubbed with candle wax or oil; (2) The marker should be only as hot as when applied to paper, the paper gets red. When these [precautions] are observed, the slaves will not suffer bad effects from the branding.[24]

The implications here are daunting. The practice of branding must in some cases have caused injuries severe enough to impair the already traumatized person in a way that threatened their monetary value. It is not clear what exactly those injuries might have been — and I'm not interested in determining them — but the fact that there was a need to issue these cautionary instructions suggests all manner of horrific results probably occurred. Some of that trauma might have been caused by the excessively intricate design of the brand, as we have already seen. Also, many Africans were forced to undergo the excruciating process more than once.[25] They might be branded DY when they were first acquired in Africa, then branded again upon arrival in the Americas under new ownership, and yet *again* if punished for a misdeed, such as running away,

24 Johannes Postma, *The Dutch in the Atlantic Slave Trade, 1600–1815* (New York: Cambridge University Press, 1990), 368.

25 Jay A. Levenson, Diogo Ramada Curto, and Jack C. Richard, eds., *Encompassing the Globe: Portugal and the World in the 16th & 17th Centuries* (Washington, D.C.: Arthur M. Sackler Gallery, Smithsonian Institution, 2007), 108.

or being persistently "disobedient" in some way. Sometimes they were branded twice at the start. Unfortunate Africans caught up in the matrix of Queen Anne and Philip V's *assiento* were branded on the back with the South Sea Company mark, as well as on the chest with the Spanish royal mark.

The sad fact is that branding enslaved Africans was a fact of slavery. It established ownership; it identified the owner as a figure of power; it framed the branded as abject objects. The correlation that we are now so familiar with is that Africans were considered living chattel, the equivalent of swine or sheep or cattle, whose purpose was to serve the needs of those placed above them in Nature's indisputable echelons. I can exult at the agency of Black cowboys who wielded brands, but I cannot ignore the fact of how branding has been used to objectify Black people. In a manner of speaking, this is *my* Double Yoke. If the brands of Black cowboys and ranchers represent an untapped language — or, as I put it earlier, an historical poetry — then this is the legacy of that language; this is what also gets spoken, what is also whispered in the archives, fleshed out in our forgettings. Because it was common to brand the company's initials onto enslaved Africans' skin. SCC (South Sea Company) and RAC (Royal African Company) were brands as recognizable in the seventeenth century as HBC is today in the twenty-first. Remembering the financial, conceptual, and legal alignments between the royal family's companies, consider how thinly the three letters of HBC today act as a layer, cutaneously light, veiling the letters RAC, hiding them from view, marking them with the silenced sound of history.

NUMINOUS ANIMAL

In some ways, the branding of Africans executed part of the process of their transformation into something less than – or, to some, *other* than – human. The conversion ushered in Blackness as the dominant framing for African humanity. In fact, Blackness dilutes African humanity; it flattens it, empties it of its natural multi-dimensionality. I have talked to many Africans who now make their home in this part of the world and who have expressed how they did not conceive of themselves as Black in any overt, self-conscious way until they came here. Upon arrival, who they are, as well as who they have been, is dramatically reconfigured: suddenly, they are implicated in the history of a country that had emerged from the shaping collision between the RAC and HBC. Now, in the Americas, on the Canadian Prairies, they are seen in natural alignment with all manner of people who up to this point have had nothing in common with them, from Shaquille O'Neal to Harriet Tubman to Drake to some random family who happens to live at the end of their street. They are pulverized in a merciless mortar only to be scraped out, forcibly reshaped into something that, apparently, can be comprehensively understood through a handful of stereotypes and repeated anecdotes. This transformation, though not nearly as brutal, is our modern equivalent of branding slaves. And though it would be unfair to say that Black people feel like the animals of North America, it would not be inaccurate to say that we are often made to feel less than human in North America.

Nonetheless, enslaved Africans who were brought to this continent were not thought of as animals in the usual sense. Yes, their humanity was denied and all manner of atrocities were visited upon them. The shocking fact is that despite their regular dehumanization they were invariably integrated (willingly or not) into the European family tree. Today, approximately one out of five African Americans has European ancestry. That's a staggeringly high number. White enslavers and overseers seemed to have no qualms about engaging in the most intimate of human relations with a category of people that were otherwise considered subhuman. Often, they had already had white wives and white children even as they had extramarital relations and produced extramarital children, essentially, in broad daylight. The women and children forced into and out of these extramarital relations often lived under the resentful gaze of the white matriarch – who had no legal or social power to refute her husband's activities – and had complicated relations with the white children of the household. It was as though this kind of heinous indulgence, though frowned upon, didn't truly count, despite – or because of – the recognized subhuman status of Black people. This is not the kind of interaction that is accepted – resentfully or not – with true animals. It helps to show the striking contradiction at the heart of Black personhood: we are people who do not count as people.

When my parents emigrated to Edmonton, Alberta from Freetown, Sierra Leone, without even knowing it they had already been reconfigured before they had arrived. I'm sure they experienced an untold number of jaw-dropping, dehumanizing encounters, but the one that was shared as a family story when I was growing up was their church debacle. Let me first remind you that Sierra Leone was founded by formerly enslaved Africans, who had been transformed into Black beings, who then forged their way back to Africa imbued with their transformations. Let me also remind you that part of those transformations involved displaying a bevy of European traits to the extent that they were accused of being Afro-Saxons, including their manner of dress, their educational system, and their religion. Let me finally remind you that so distinctly did they espouse their religious identity that other Africans, who found themselves in Freetown but had not been similarly transformed by slavery's merciless mortar, called them *Akiriyo* in their language because they seemed so often to be going to church. All of this, I will finally add, was established in the late 1700s, long before Albertan churchgoers were even a thing, long before Alberta was even a thing, before Canada itself was even a thing.

For my parents newly arrived in Edmonton, then, attending church was a consideration that was not even a consideration in the way that breathing is a consideration that is not even a consideration for all of us. Their families had been attending Christian churches for nearly two centuries. My mother came from a family of staunch Anglicans dating from Sierra Leone's earliest colonial period, and my father's family were Methodists whose name (Bickersteth) was carved into one of the foundational stones of their church. My dad had even started down the path of becoming a pastor before he married my mom and their trajectory changed as they became immigrants instead.

When they attended church in Edmonton, they were welcomed, but there was an unfamiliar vibe. To their confusion, the pastor launched into a sermon about heathens in Africa who needed prayers, who needed to learn about the light of Jesus Christ to save them from the darkness of their pagan continent. "They are not evil people," the pastor intoned, "they are simply ignorant of Christ's path. They are not blessed in the same way as us and so they need us; they need our prayers to show them the light they cannot see." My parents looked at each other, blinking. They had arrived in Edmonton in September, so I imagine a slice of early-autumn morning light suddenly hitting their eyes. I would have been barely two months old at the time. Was I there with them? Did I suddenly and inexplicably start wailing as babies do when you least want them to? It was a moment.

It was a moment that scarred my parents who could not conceive of a God who would allow Christian people to be so ignorant of another part of the Christian world. It scarred them badly enough that they stopped going to church for years to come. But scars are the result of a previous wounding. And in this case, the wound was the contradiction of Black personhood. These Edmontonian churchgoers believed they were extending sympathy to fellow human beings. At the same time, they could not conceive of fellow human beings in Africa sharing a type of humanity that was common to them. To them – and to many people today – Africa has no meaningful history; hence, it couldn't possibly already have Christians; it *must* need saving. Because there is no scope for it in this discussion, and because I really hope we're past this stage by now, I am just going to skip over the fact of Africa's multi-millennial Christian presence or the white saviour complex so obviously in evidence here.

This experience marked my parents' initiation into North American Blackness, a state in which one's historical realities – both personal and social – are no longer considered real; in which one's dimensionality is flattened to one or two tones; in which this strange Blackness, which is not even a colour, colours everything about how one is perceived; in which the stories generated about Blackness limit one's possibilities to the point of refuting any meaningful tomorrow. You thought you were a human being like other human beings, but it turns out, on this continent, you are *like* a human being, in the way that a cherished cat or dog – or any other variety of creature that is valued akin to kin – is *like* a human. This is your new status as a person. It is not just scary, it is scarring. Something is gouged from you, or dismantles you, or lacerates you in a damaging and lasting way. Your humanness is opened up and then scored and then thickens and solidifies around itself. You feel yourself become a scar and then you understand why everyone else looks at you in the way they do. You are not a person like they are. You were never meant to be a person like they are on this continent. You are the walking wound of their ambitions. And your Blackness will never go away because they need it; they need your scarified personhood as proof of their own belonging. As the refuse in stratified Western modernity, Black people are the needed unnecessaries. Honestly, there's never been another kind of animal like us before.

I would like to suggest a numinous quality to scarified animals and persons alike. Today, no one argues that forcibly applying a superheated rod of iron metal to a human being's bare flesh is not an inhuman act. But it is a conundrum that an act of inhumanity on one group could, at one point, somehow, be realized as the proof of humanity of the other. In part, this conundrum reflects a straightforward point that James Baldwin made often regarding exploitative racism. Here is one such example:

> If [white] Americans were not so terrified of their private selves, they would never have needed to invent and could never have become so dependent on what they still call 'the Negro problem.' This problem, which they invented in order to safeguard their purity, has made of them criminals and monsters.[26]

On the other side of things, though, a separate argument has emerged regarding the application of this same heated iron to the flesh of cattle. Ranchers have long been the target of animal rights activists who assert that branding cattle is a barbaric practice that causes undue and unwarranted suffering on the animal. Lest I mislead you into believing there is a stark division between people who support animal rights and people who raise animals for food production, the division is not always so neat: many farmers and ranchers care deeply about the animals they raise and regularly

26 James Baldwin, *No Name in the Street*, First Vintage International Edition (New York: Vintage Books, 2007), 54.

seek ways to avoid or alleviate suffering. Where the two groups may actually diverge is in their understanding of personhood, who gets to be associated with personhood, and what natural rights are conferred with personhood.

Baldwin's quote, like so much of what he writes, offers brilliant insight into the Blackness we seek to escape and the Blackness to which we are ineluctably joined. Baldwin is a subtle thinker, though, and whiteness is often also implicated in his arguments around conceptions of Blackness. In "Down at the Cross: Letter from a Region in My Mind," he elaborates that "whatever white people do not know about Negroes reveals, precisely and inexorably, what they do not know about themselves."[27] Then he complicates *this* thought when he refers to his Blackness as a barrier between him and himself, which he characterizes as both an affliction and, crucially, a crutch.[28] At the heart of all of these words is his complex reckoning with self. White society must reckon with Blackness as a solipsism of its own making; Black people must reckon with Blackness as a socially-constructed self that therefore demands self-*critique*.

Here's a trivial but appropriate way of thinking of it. All my life I have been a dog lover and have never really appreciated cats. My wife, on the other hand, grew up with a cat as a family pet, and for a period of my married life I found myself living with two cats.

---

27 James Baldwin, *The Fire Next Time*, First Vintage International Edition (New York: Vintage Books, 1993), 44.

28 James Baldwin, *Nobody Knows My Name*, First Vintage International Edition (New York: Vintage Books, 1993), xi–xii.

While I never understood the overall appeal of cats, I did eventually find myself liking one of them. Later in life, through a variety of circumstances, we shifted to dogs and my wife (I am happy to say) changed camps. She now thoroughly prefers dogs. Our current dog is a very intelligent Giant Schnauzer who has a playful but dominating spirit. I find many things about him unusual in striking and impressive ways, but I'm not sure I *like* him. So, I am a dog lover who doesn't like his own dog. But I think I recognize that a lot of this has to do with my sense of self rather than his particular personality quirks. I love dogs, but it's clear to me that I prefer dogs who reinforce my sense of superiority. To some extent, I think this is why all dog-lovers love dogs. They shower us with adoration and, for the most part, they show obedience to our will. Who wouldn't love that? It's almost like being a god.

But we're not gods. We are human beings split between feelings of self-abnegation and self-absorption. Two summers ago this became clear to me when my dog changed colours. Let me explain. Otto is a Giant Schnauzer with a wilful, dominating personality, but he is also very playful and affectionate in an energetic, uncompromising way. At off-leash parks, he is the dog that boldly leads the walk roughly a hundred feet ahead of me, announcing his presence and asserting himself with whomever he approaches. But folks love him. He never lets them pass without dancing in circles in front of them, forcing his head beneath their hands, stealing happy caresses from them. Of course, they never see it like that. I'm the one framing it as theft (remember?). He can be manipulative, though, and his main pleasure comes from displacing another dog from their human companion. That is a large part of the exuberant petting he seeks. If the dog approaches him while he is being pet, he will bark loudly at them and chase them away. Then he returns happily for more petting. For some reason, nobody sees this but me (and the displaced dogs). Otto, my Giant Schnauzer with the giant personality, remains as popular as ever with the other dog walkers.

Until the summer he changed colours. To be clear, Otto is a black dog, like most Giant Schnauzers. But last summer he had to undergo dental surgery. As part of the healing process, he had to wear a muzzle to prevent him from biting or chewing on anything that could rupture his stitches. To my surprise, everyone started treating him differently. Now he received wide-eyed stares from a distance. When he approached others with his usual exuberance, they avoided him. One person, who hadn't noticed his muzzle at first, happily stretched a hand toward him, and then, just as he reached her, suddenly veered in the other direction. The few people who would pause to greet him, would very cautiously touch him, or hold their hands away from him altogether. A few rogues, who I will never forget, seemed not to notice the muzzle at all, and gave Otto exactly the rough love that he always sought, turning and turning in happy circles as they rubbed him vigorously. Very few people even asked about the muzzle, but simply responded to some script they had in their minds. To my surprise, I found myself volunteering the information, defensively, protectively, before anyone had a chance to judge him: "He's fine; it's a preventative measure while his mouth heals from surgery." The explanation always broke the unspoken tension and Otto got his rubs, albeit cautiously.

One summer evening we were out walking; a family with small children stopped in their tracks when they saw Otto, the parents pulling the kids close to them. They gave me tight smiles as we passed them (I kept Otto leashed by me). Suddenly, without any warning, it occurred to me what I had been missing all along: *my black dog had become a Black dog.* I looked back at the family we had passed, the kids laughing and leaping about with their coiffed Spaniel, who had actually cowered at Otto's approach, everyone's blond hair shimmering and shining as the light of the evening sun faded. I turned back to Otto, who was trotting up to the next group of dog walkers, oblivious. And then, again, I surprised myself with another thought: no, not *oblivious*, but undaunted. Otto was unstoppable in his confidence, his sense of purpose, and his vision for achieving what he wanted in the world. I felt the usual cautionary words tickle the back of my throat, ready to launch before the dog walkers veered away from him: "He's fine." But I didn't. He *is* fine. He is completely unchanged from who he was before the muzzle, before he became *Black*. In fact, he has always been a B/black dog. This may even be the crux of Blackness. It is attached to us, regardless of our actual, intrinsic nature. Otto was bold before. Now he was Black and bold. He was assertive. Now he was Black and assertive. He sought to control the narrative. Now he was Black and controlling. He was an animal before, but now he had become a Black animal, a numinous animal. In this way, he was utterly changed although he had not changed in the least. What's more, he made no apologies for his Blackness. The problem was me. It had always been me. I had felt defensive about this dog that I originally didn't like because I sensed an affinity with his Blackness. Now, I resented the fact that my first instinct had been to appease others, relieve *them* of their imagined fears. I completely changed tack after that. I stopped seeing him through other people's eyes. *I* stopped seeing his muzzle. I admired his indifference at other people's preconceptions. I loved his undaunted determination to demand love that he deserved. He became wholly likeable to me. I shifted entirely; he made me feel good about myself.

And then, a few weeks later, when the muzzle came off, I shifted back again. Without changing a single thing about himself, he reverted to being manipulative, forceful, thieving. How could this happen? It happened because I'm not a God. I'm a human. And that means being split between self-abnegation and self-absorption: we all are when it comes to our dogs. Or maybe we are like Greek gods. We shift our allegiances (from dogs to cats to dogs) when it suits us. And it happens to suit us most when we find ourselves forced to confront that side of us that is exploitative, that measures love in degrees of how it mirrors what we want to see. We carry a split on the surface of who we are: is our love empathetic or apathetic? Are we protective over our dogs, or do they "safeguard our purity," as Baldwin says? This split of who we are is a scar. Blackness is a scar and scars us. In my parents' case, the encounter with the Blackness that North America forced on them changed them dramatically, socially, and personally. I also suspect that there was something in them that *didn't* change, that maybe they had already been questioning some aspect of their faith. In fact, to this day I would describe them as questioning people; that is, they are both curious individuals who are interested in exploring questions and reconsidering their lives in reflection of their questioning. You might say that the imposition of Blackness brought out the Blackness in them. But I prefer to see it differently. Their doubts were viewed as Black doubts; their loss of faith as Black loss; the disruption of their questioning as Black rupture. This is James Baldwin's double reckoning. It is Green Walters's Double Yoke. Socially, they were Africans who became reinvented as Black people, whose role and status differed from what they had previously known, as well as from everyone else's. Personally, they were deeply affected; their Christian faith was damaged. I can only imagine that they felt betrayed by their God, the God they had known and loved for so much of their lives, so much so that my father was going to become a pastor. The result of this damage is that they stopped going to church, and not just for a short while. I essentially grew up in an agnostic household (my dad had turned atheist, but my mother held on to certain rituals) and almost never set foot in a church until I was fifteen years old. They eventually did return to their Christian faith, but, as I said, it took years. They had been scarred.

NUMINOUS ANAMNESIS

The reconfiguring of Africa led to a reconfiguring of Africans in a scarring way. Our histories became collapsed into one amorphous relationship with Europe and the West. But this too is what allows for a relating between us. My parents arrive and are scarred.

I grow up here, scarred. Green Walters and John Ware invent cattle brand designs that are inherently scarred. And all of us make choices that are also impossible returns. In this way, the history of Black cowboys on the Prairies – a history that is not directly related to my personal or family history – becomes intimately part of my history. One might argue that someone like Cheryl Foggo, whose ancestors formed the spine of Alberta's pioneering history, has a legitimate claim over a figure like John Ware, whereas I am merely clutching at straws. I don't begrudge Cheryl's claim on this history one bit. At the same time, though, I recognize that we both access this history in a similar way: the repudiation of the common flattening of our humanness. In our case, the flattening is specifically achieved through the erasure of a crucial historical contribution to this part of the world. We can't forget that everyone except for Indigenous people migrated here at some point. When it comes to people of African descent, that migration is activated by a scarring Blackness, which is then reactivated upon arrival. Cheryl's Blackness was activated with the arrival of her ancestors in the early 1900s. John Ware's was activated with his arrival in the late 1800s. Mine was activated when my parents arrived in that church pew in 1969. Because we are each forced to confront this flattening-Blackness as a consequence of forced migrations and arrivals, we all have access to the commonality of each other's histories, though they are not common.

This brings me to my own very specific approach for confronting the flattening of Blackness, my own scars, and the commonly experienced erasure of Black history in this part of the world.

At the heart of it is the language of Black cowboys. I am a poet. I work with words. Mainly, I use words to try to recover and reclaim historic Black presences that have gone missing. As I have shown several times, it is our national and regional default to evacuate the historical memory of Black presence, and this happens in very specific ways: we do not learn of community building, or enterprise, or ingenuity, or intelligence, or aspiration, or love. When we learn about historical Black presences in this part of the world – if we learn about them at all – we are invariably enveloped in stories that demonstrate lack of agency, singularity, physical heroics/atrocities, criminal exploits, or undifferentiated presences. It is the most normal thing in the world to dismiss or ignore or simply discount the variegated, dimensioned existence of Black people in this part of the world. It is one of the things that draws me to ally myself with Indigenous causes here, as this is a social position that they share with Black communities.

My goal, then, was to find a way, using words, to counter these tendencies. Poetry is often my go-to tool because poetry can so effectively fill in the gaps of what we don't or can't know. For example, when it comes to understanding John Ware's brand, we can only speculate because Ware left no specific explanations about his choices in writing or in discussion with others. Poetry allows us to speculate in a way that both reimagines Ware's story, and at the same time exposes the limitation of the conventional interpretations of his connections to slavery and his "lucky" number. One of the poems I published in *filling Station* engages this process. As I said, the language of cattle brands is at the heart of my approach, but my aim is to effect something more than just reproducing a forgotten brand (as important as that is). I want to expose a contestable relationship with the past that has largely been seen as given. The poem consists of words that are arranged in the shape of Ware's "Walking Sticks" brand. The title of the poem is very long and effectively acts as a portion of the poem itself. I will reproduce it for you here:

Some say they're walking sticks, some say they're nines, some say nine was his lucky number because of something to do with slavery and freedom and some connection to the number nine, and some say he was born in Texas, and some say they're just walking sticks

unknown un
unknown known
unknown unknown
unknown unknown
unknown unknown
unknown unknown
unknown unknown
unknown unknown
unknown unknown
unknown
unknown
unknown
unknown
unknown
unknown
unknown

John Ware is one of the most documented Black people we have in our Prairie history. There is no other Black figure for whom we have accumulated so much recorded evidence. In part, this is why you have never heard of other Black cowboys like Thomas Rife, Lige Abel, or Green Walters. Not only did those Black men

FIG 6 "Some Say..." by Bertrand Bickersteth.

not have any access to the recording instruments of history to instantiate their own stories, but the "mainstream" keepers of history only thought to include them as footnotes or accessories – if they thought to include them at all – to what they deemed as "proper" history. By comparison, John Ware is practically buried in historical accounts. Yet, as you can see from my poem, what we don't know about Ware far outweighs what we do. When it comes to Black history, being buried in a deluge of accounts guarantees very little factual accounting of a person's dimensionality.

Another poem, "A Black Hand Revisits," adds a layer – dimensionality – to the effect achieved in "Some say. . ." This time, a poem is presented in the conventional sense, with multiple lines of evocative words, figuring some meaningful representation for the reader. But there is an added feature:

A Black Hand Revisits

A black hand revi**sits, wrinkles,** flesh and folds
rolling up agai**nst the foothills of a** learned
language, **grasp**s at *el idioma* ***de los*** *vaqueros*,
lingers in ***el len****guaje del cuer***po. How** much of
your stub**born** history persist**s in the** *maneras*
of [our] ma**nners**, subarct**ic? A cer**tain equili-
brium on horseback. An **easing** shift of weight
in sympathy with the **[beast] b**elow. A light flick
of the wrist, unwrest**ling the** encircling, the *lazo*,
around *esta lengu***a. And.** How much of Black
Atlantica lives i**n your p**hysical script? *Pampas*
to plains. Pla**ins to pr**airie. Black Cowboy.
Black *Vaq****uero.*** **B**lack *Gaucho. Conquistador.*
*Cuerpo te****rco.*** **Wh**ite *noise*
rescript**ed by h**and.

FIG 7 "A Black Hand Revisits" by Bertrand Bickersteth.

The strategic use of bold formatting combined with the grey shading of the text produces a layered effect. Over top of the conventional poem, itself concerned with wrinkles, folds, and surfaces – as much of the land as of the flesh – is Ware's "walking stick" brand. John Ware's intellectual and imaginative presence, his economic acumen, his visible agency is the extra dimension of this poem. It is, for me, a way of returning Ware to contemporary relevance from the abyss of national amnesia where much of Black history on the Prairies lives, where Blackness itself is flattened to an inhuman proportion. But let me remind you of the Double Yoke of poetic agency. Yes, it is important for me to incorporate cattle brands in these poems – even recognizing the horrific history of their application to enslaved Africans – but central to these brands, in the particularity of their Black historicity (which cannot hold the reins of its own narration as readily as the dominant eurocentric version so candidly does) is that they are riddled with gaps; there is always an aspect that remains elusive. It is not even possible to know for certain what Ware's brand *is*. The number nine? A walking stick? So, this is the dimensionality that I have added. This is the "extra" layer that fleshes out Ware's life for us: an unknowability. But, also, this is clearly a palimpsestic uncovering: something gets covered over even as we rescue Ware's dimensionality. In this way, I am poeticizing a common distorting that occurs in memorializing Ware. In a discussion related to my point, Karina Vernon, Canada's pre-eminent scholar on Black Prairie literature, reveals how John Ware's memorial at Dinosaur Provincial Park covers up the wider context of his presence – the Black communities he circulated in — for the sake of a white-washed mythology about his singularity. "As a way of remembering John Ware," she points out, "this memorial only forgets."[29] In other words, covering over is a key feature in the meaning-making of John Ware. Likewise, if we are to take the "meaning" of Ware's brand in the poem "Some say. . ." and juxtapose it with visual effect of "A Black Hand," yet another layer, another accretion of meaning, is produced through the Black cowboy's signature mark. That is, over top of everything — or undergirding everything from below — is the inescapability of *unknown*.

Over the summer of 2025, I had the privilege of joining an archaeological dig on the site of John Ware's original cabin near Millarville, AB. Reputedly, the site has been unoccupied since Ware and his family lived there over a century ago. However, time having worked its forces, no one was certain of the exact location, nor if anything at all from that period had survived. Cheryl Foggo had initiated this work several years ago, and it partly informed her documentary, *John Ware Reclaimed*. A few tantalizing objects were uncovered, suggesting the likely possibility that his original residence was indeed very nearby, and a summer of speculative digging, turned into a federal grant, a team of archaeologists, and a multi-year exploration of the area. Cheryl invited me to join the latest phase of the project and I had the pleasure of being introduced to actual archaeological work by an actual archaeologist,

29 Karina Vernon, "The Black Prairies: History, Subjectivity, Writing" (PhD diss., University of Victoria, 2008), 3.

Lindsay Amundsen-Meyer, the project leader. True archaeology necessitates none of the antics we know of Indiana Jones, so-called archaeologist, who spends most of his time running, jumping, escaping, wooing, or looking harried and – other than very brief instances in each film – almost no time digging. I also can't help adding that he is not very scientific in his approach, nor is he an ethical archaeologist, often stealing objects and disregarding or dismissing sovereign Indigenous rights, cultural, or traditional claims.

True archaeology is methodical and precise. An area of land is carefully selected after intensive assessments that might involve advanced technology, like GIS analysis, magnetometry, and Ground Penetrating Radar (now widely associated with a different history of perpetuated horrors: the grim tragedy of locating hitherto unidentified Indigenous burial sites at former residential schools). Then, when a specific dig location is determined, standard "low" tech takes over: an area is marked off and precisely laid out in a grid; the soil is removed in layers, sometimes as thin as a few centimetres at a time; as excavation progresses, each grid unit is inventoried assiduously – even obsessively – so that the precise location and context (what archaeologists call the *provenience*) of every find is documented, often by plotting it within the site grid or by triangulation from fixed datum points. Even the chemical composition of the soil is analyzed to give a clear understanding of its potential impact on the human-hewn artifacts that it has suspended for decades, or centuries, or longer. Each excavated level is also passed through a screen as microartifacts and organic remains are often missed by the naked eye. This work carries on layer by layer, unit by unit (or each square of the grid), until it reaches sterile soil, or, equally, a story begins to emerge.

I was enchanted to learn that this process of uncovering, layer by layer, the stories hidden in the soil is known as stratigraphy to archaeologists. To a writer, it seemed like such a beautifully appropriate way of expressing the methodology involved: the writing (-graphy) or composition of a story through its uncovering in layers (strata). Beautiful. I was lucky in other ways too. On the day I visited the site, the weather was beautiful, the sky endlessly blue; it was sunny and warm. The wet weather we had been experiencing for much of the summer would continue later that month, but on that day the worst thing to contend with was the mosquitoes. Honestly, even the outhouse on site was practically pleasant. These auspicious conditions were perhaps the marks of the dig's success on the whole. In previous years, a few promising items had been identified. This year, they hit the jackpot. Lindsay grinned up at me from the bottom of the excavation pit where she pointed out significant features they had located beneath the surface. She wiped a streak of dirt from her forehead and urged me into the pit beside her. There, she pointed to the stratigraphic layers, which revealed the cross-section of a decomposed sunken floor. She pointed out cut nails (or square machine-cut nails) that had been found, which specifically associated the site chronology with John Ware's contemporaneous period. Beyond the pit, she showed me items such as a thimble, an ink bottle, and other items that also positively identified the time period as contemporaneous with the Ware family's. We climbed out of the pit and she continued the story beyond. Here, she pointed out, is the trace of the irrigation system that Ware had constructed behind his property. And here, she said, is the refuse pit where bones that had been gnawed by the family dog(s) were recovered. And items like this, she emphasized, indicating the thimble, are evidence of Mildred Ware, John's wife, of her particular influence on the family environment, on family life on the prairie. Wow, I thought. That sunken floorboard had me floored. "All of this," Lindsay asserted, "is the evidence of John Ware and his family's living and enduring presence on this land." Despite the persistent absence of Black communities in Prairie history, despite the inevitable flattening of their dimensionality whenever we are graced a glimpse of them, the story that is told in these strata that Lindsay read for me demonstrates otherwise. I was overwhelmed.

I like to think of poems like "Some say. . ." and my poetic project as being akin to stratigraphy, but in a very special way. While archaeologists "read" through history by uncovering layers of soil, poetic stratigraphy *recovers* lost history palimpsestically. With this type of poetry, the act of uncovering *is* the act of covering. Or the result of *dis*-covery is, to put it poetically, the process of *this covery*. This, to some extent, is the role of art where other disciplines – science, law, religion – fail us. Even though we might be able to determine a historical fact to a specific and narrow degree of certainty, the uncertain factor always remains. The arts, and in my case, poetry, deliver that elusive part of the fact, the irretrievable unknown, even as it reinforces – irretrievably – the unknown.

THE BROKEN LANGUAGE OF BLACK COWBOYS

As I mentioned earlier, I never liked the name Bertrand as a child. My father named me after the philosopher and mathematician Bertrand Russell, probably, because he was attracted to his intellectual achievements. But outside of the academic circles my father moved in, Bertrand Russell was an unknown quantity, especially in the Edmonton, Alberta of my childhood. When I was younger and still being buffeted about by opposing gravitational wells of the twin stars that raised me, I was self-conscious about anything that exposed me as anomalous. So I was quick to suggest "Bert" as a neutralizing familiar when people stumbled over it. In combination with my triple-syllable alliterative mouthful of a last name, "Bertrand" felt like an over-the-top, musical-theatre move toward something far-flung and foreign.

Like most children of immigrants, I was completely occupied with trying to convince the wider white world of my environs that I was just as normal as they were. The irony is that although I settled on the placating, single-syllable version of my name ("Bert"), and although that *did* solve the problem of having a confusing name, when my Prairie African relatives joined the bandwagon – as immigrants always do – the single syllable of my name became something different. Somehow, it sounded even more simple – simplistic even – against the hinted background of an unwanted cornucopia. It came out as "Bat," which should have echoed benignly with baseball, or a vampire's alter ego;

instead, it emphasized an African relief against a Lawrence Welk soundscape, the single pulse teeming with Fela Kuti's affluence of Afrobeat. To be clear, in my teenage world neither relief was a relief. This was typical of the inward contestations I endured with identity: whenever I didn't get the thing I wanted, I was unhappy; whenever I got the thing I wanted, I didn't get the thing I wanted.

Today, my view is entirely different and I cherish those so-called mispronunciations of my name. I no longer even see them as mispronunciations (because they're *not*). I see them as the most legitimate expression of who I am: a Canadian of African descent whose second cousin is history. It was unfair of me to understand my African culture as one of thievery; that is, as a culture that lacked its own indigenous origins. But, as you now know, I didn't arrive at that understanding accidentally or voluntarily. Like everyone else, I had a hard time seeing any meaningful tomorrow in the script that had been legated to me. My perceptions were limited to these dead-end narratives. I didn't hear the inherent poetry in Krio. I didn't hear the inherent poetry in my Uncle Biola's or any of my African relatives' playful uttering of my name. Instead, I heard an English that was broken. What I could not have known is that accessing and inheriting the legacy of a broken language would teach me to be an uncommon listener. And that would eventually teach me to be a poet.

Today, I teach at a college whose athletics teams are called Broncos. In the past, I may have felt alienated and somewhat dismissed by this name. But now that I have done more than just scratch the surface of Black history here in Alberta, I have extensive knowledge of multiple ways in which these tropes — conventionally reserved for white people — were never, factually and historically, occupied exclusively by white people. Black cowboys have been the greatest preserve of my sense of historical belonging in this regard. Today, when I hear one of my students refer to the Broncos, or I see a post from the Broncos Athletics social media team, I smile to myself. I have learned about African horse and cattle traditions. I have followed the life of Kareem Rosser, a Black professional polo player from Philadelphia. I know of an entire team of Black polo players at Morehouse, Martin Luther King's alma mater. I regularly explore the buried historic presence of Black cowboys and horsemen, people like Billy Welsh, James Whitford, the Robinsons (a father and son duo), and multiple members of the Lewis family, including Ethel Alice Lewis, Spencer Lewis, and Nettie Ware, John and Mildred's daughter. Now when one of my students refers to the Broncos, I feel the term belongs to me in a way that I know they would never suspect. To put it bluntly, one of the things that John Ware was famous for was riding broncos. He had excellent horsemanship skills. If there was a horse that needed breaking, John was capable of subduing it. There is a famous story that Grant MacEwan tells in his biography of John Ware in which an unsuspecting crew of ranch hands attempt to have a good laugh at Ware's expense by cajoling him into riding what they knew to be one of the orneriest horses on the ranch. John, who is quietly certain of his skills, plays along, reluctantly agreeing to do it if they will give him an improved saddle to the one he currently had. The famous, much-repeated line is, "If you give me a little better saddle, and a little worse horse, I think I can ride him."[30] Everyone happily agrees, rubbing their hands in anticipation of Ware being tossed onto his backside. To their shock, Ware sticks in the saddle, calmly and expertly wearing the horse down until "the once-famous bucking horse stood in subdued quiet."[31] The ranch hands stare, blinking, and Ware wins a new saddle.

It's hard to know how accurate this story is given that so much of MacEwan's text was gleaned from oral histories. But I'm sure there's an element of truth to it. Ware was absolutely known for his horsemanship, so even if this story didn't exactly happen, the point of the story did. One joy I get from this story is how "breaking" becomes something good here, becomes a sign of mastery, of expertise, and even belonging. Once Ware demonstrated his abilities to the others, everything changed. They rightfully produced the saddle for him and bestowed an enduring sense of respect on him from that day forward. He was clearly one of them. "Breaking" brought them together. Maybe even more importantly, I love how this story shows his agency. For once, we see a Black man in a position of mastery and authority over his situation. The ranch hands thought they knew what a Black man was capable of (being flattened), but Ware knew differently and was given the chance to show it. He *chose* his action and ended up the better for it. I love that choosing.

---

30 Grant MacEwan, *John Ware's Cow Country* (Edmonton: Institute of Applied Art, Ltd., 1960), 46.
31 MacEwan, *John Ware's Cow Country*, 47.

Had I had the sense to listen to the lesson of Krio's poetry when I was younger, I would have seen that what I thought of as "broken" was the sign of mastery, of expertise. Of course, that was impossible for me as a teenager. But when I was older, I did learn to see that mastery. I did learn to hear the expertise of a culture's redeployment of language. I mentioned earlier that there are connections between the Krio word *bɔbɔ* and the English word *bọy*. To my teenage ears, I could not hear any difference at all (even though, in this case, the words do not even have the same number of syllables). The two are only distantly connected. In this same distant way, though, the word *bọy* also harbours an unexpected connection to the word *cowbọy*.

There is some speculation that the word *cowbọy* actually betrays the presence of Black labourers on ranches and cattle trails and roundups. The logic is as follows: while there were many different words to identify someone who worked with cattle, on a ranch or on a trail – for example, cowhand, ranch hand, cowpoke, cowpuncher, and cowboy – the word *boy* was largely used for Black men, regardless of age or expertise.[32] Remember, the era of cowboys was not very long but it did briefly overlap with slavery. We tend to think of enslaved Africans forced into labour on southern plantations, but truthfully, enslaved Africans were used anywhere that hard labour was required. So if you owned a ranch, and you

---

32 This happened in Canada too. See, for example, Stanley G. Grizzle, *My Name's Not George: The Story of the Brotherhood of Sleeping Car Porters* (Toronto: Umbrella Press, 1998), 39.

owned slaves, you would put those enslaved people to work on your ranch. They would gain all of the skills that any working ranch hand would need to develop and in many cases they would develop them to a very high degree because they were made to do the hardest, most technically demanding tasks. In Texas, where ranching and slavery were particularly common, many people who worked with cattle were Indigenous, Black, or Mexican. In fact, they were so numerous that no one racial group held a majority, including cowboys of European descent.[33] So the prevalence of Black men in the industry makes it probable that the word *boy* as a term addressing them was also prevalent. While a term like ranch *hand* may have referred to anyone working on the ranch, cow*boy* was very likely reserved for Black men.[34]

This is the kind of poetry that history hides that I have learned to listen for. The Double Yoke of this poetry in history is also always present. For, hiding behind the word *cowboy* are two joined problems, two joined revelations. On the one hand, we uncover the previously obscured presence of Black contributions in an area that is conventionally understood as dominated by the agency and concerns of white people. On the other hand, we once more *dis*-cover

33 David Goldstein-Shirley, "Black Cowboys in the American West: An Historiographical Review," *Ethnic Studies Review* 20 (1997): 86.

34 See Maria C. Hunt, "'A History That's Been Suppressed': The Black Cowboy Story Is 200 Years Old," *The Guardian*, 19 May 2024, https://www.theguardian.com/culture/ng-interactive/2024/may/19/black-cowboys-cowgirls-rodeos; and, Mike A. Mroz, "Black Cowboys of the Cattle Frontier," *Legacy* 16, no. 1 (2016): 12n16, https://opensiuc.lib.siu.edu/legacy/vol16/iss1/3.

the relegation of Blackness to some flattened entity without choice or agency: regardless of one's level of expertise or experience, regardless of whether one is seventeen or seventy-two, being a Black male meant one was perennially subservient, underdeveloped, unworthy of stature; in short, it meant one was trapped in the perpetuity of boyhood.

I suppose I sensed this when I was a teenager, when I instinctively reacted against it by giving in to the stereotype of thievery. When you are a recognizable thief, you feel diminished, relegated to a lower status, certainly, but you also feel like a master of certain otherwise elusive limitations. The rules that contain you, and everyone else to a large extent, do not apply to you, even as they are applied to you. In a contradictory way, I felt more *adult* as a thief, and this is a feeling that most teenagers struggle to realize; it is what we yearn for almost more than anything else and is why we start smoking and drinking and seeking sexual encounters with verve. I say in a "contradictory" way because this feeling of adulthood I was experiencing was in tension with another, very different context that was being imposed on me.

As a youngster, I was largely seen as an oddity by other Albertans. My presence was questioned, the whiteness of my palms was remarked upon, and people took liberties with my hair; these things made me feel embarrassed and deeply uncomfortable, but nothing was as confusing as the treatment I received from a certain category of young, white women before I hit puberty. Generally, they fawned over me. I was coddled and cuddled. My cheeks were pinched. My pre-puberty chub was squeezed. I was the target of uninhibited feminine giggling. I was compared to Gary Coleman, star of the seventies sitcom *Different Strokes*, in which he played a cute, chubby-cheeked Black child who, along with his older brother, was adopted by a wealthy white man. It was my Negro Teddy Bear phase, one half of the role of *boy* that had been prepared for me. When I crossed into puberty, things changed, seemingly overnight. My presence was questioned in menacing ways. Shop owners followed me in their aisles. Elderly women scowled at me on the bus and claimed the empty seat next to them with their purse or their hand. Teenage white boys who I didn't know picked fights with me, as though I was some sort of scourge or conquest. And young white women abruptly started to ignore me. This is the other half of the role of *boy*, the one that forcibly relegates. And let's be clear, this particular relegation strategically denies the Black male body as a sexual being. The threat of sexual violence – entirely invented by the white imagination – is defused in the gesture of a single, emasculating word.

The thing about these roles that were assigned to me is that I had no choice in the matter. From the cheek-pinching fawning to the hooded-eyed glaring, it was all directed at me without my having done anything. I was like Otto with a muzzle, but unlike Otto, who was indifferent to his Blackness, I struggled but couldn't fully understand these symbols that were being used to invoke me. Pre-puberty, it was a confusing, secret language that white people around me all seemed to understand and deploy amongst themselves with panache and fluency. When my friend Gabriel swept those four bottles of Polo off the shelf and into his bag, he too seemed to be speaking this same secret language to me. So when I too began to claim bottles of Polo and Lacoste pins and Jordache belts for myself, I felt myself to be accessing that language as well. At the same time, I felt like I was exposing myself to something, that this language was as dangerous as it was liberating. I wasn't sure why, but it seemed to be offering something different to Gabriel than it was offering to me. I clung to it, though, because the thing it did present to me was choice. Being a thief was a choice that being a teddy bear (or a sexual threat) was not.

When Black cowboys chose cattle brands of their own design, they too were exercising a secret language: the broken language of slave chattels. The language of choice, of choosing, particularly in a flattening world, is the counter to that flattening. But this language is only effective because it is broken and even after it breaks, it continues breaking. That is its Double Yoke: it is broken and it breaks. If I saw Krio as only broken English when I was younger, it is because I could not see that it was this very brokenness that, at the same time, made it more than English. It *breaks* English and in so doing speaks the realities of its own Africanness – its history, its culture, its music – with poetry. It does not destroy English. It does not obliterate it. Most importantly, it does not replace it. But in breaking it, Krio is able to achieve that fundamental realization of who we are: figures of the impossible return.

For Black cowboys, the language of cattle brands must always court the impossible return. This is why John Ware's brand is read as reflective of slavery and resists that reflection at the same time. This is why Green Walters's brand *is* the Double Yoke. In some ways, knowing about these Black cowboys when I was younger would have offered me a lifeline, a very different kind from the one that shoplifting seemed to be presenting. There was some instinct in me that understood things were not being presented as they were. This was years before Jim Carrey emerged on the comedy scene, years before I would start to recognize something familiar in his singular whiteness on the show *In Living Color*. It was years before he starred in the *Truman Show*, in which his character would learn that he had been living a lie, that his life was simply a series of superficial TV sets, that behind the set, an entirely different reality was playing itself out. But both versions of Jim Carrey's characters — singular whiteness and superficial reality — are important metaphors. It recently occurred to me that if everything had just been spelled out before me in plain letters, I would not have needed to become a thief. At the same time, spelling everything out was both the solution and the problem I needed to overcome. Somehow, this is exactly what every Black cowboy understood. This is what every Black cowboy's brand does. And then it hit me: exactly what I needed to do.

PART 4

FONTS OF KNOWLEDGE

THE FONT OF YESTERDAY

I needed to spell everything out in a way that I was not capable of when I was young, in a way that the Prairies and all of Canada — all of North America — is not capable of, but has always inherently had the capacity for, from its soil composition, to its vegetation, to the swirl of grasses that rollick its contours, to the living beings that graze those grasses, to the patterns of swirls they follow, to the trails of purpose we echo, to the language of that echo we emblazon in our dreams.

In following one particular trail of purpose, society has erased Black history on the Prairies. The history of Black cowboys has been removed from our consciousness. Because Blackness has flattened the possibility of a livable, ongoing tomorrow, and, paradoxically, because we live in a future tense that is so far removed from the cowboy period, it is hard to imagine any connections between the two. Everything about the Black cowboy's existence was lived in the body. They lived physical realities out in natural surroundings, where they were continuously in congregation with the herds of their concern. Almost all of the descriptions of John Ware and Green Walters and others focused on their physicality: whether it was their superhuman strength (Ware) or their subhuman proportions (Walters), or their numinous animality, the fact of their Blackness itself was defining. Today, we live lives that are removed from our physical surroundings; rather, we deny the physicality of our surroundings, often measuring success in our ability to exceed or manipulate the limits of our physicality.

We built cities conceived apart from nature. We raised buildings into the sky. We shifted the value of production from manufacturing to service to information. The trajectory continues in the technological economies of our society. Entire universes exist in our handheld devices; we continue our denial of the physical by turning more and more inward, barely noticing the world around us. At the same time, many of us *feel* more connected to the world, the wider world that was inaccessible to us pre-internet. We access music from anywhere in the world at any time we want at a tap of the finger. There is no need to visit a record store and withstand the scrutinizing disdain of the salespeople working there. We receive news notifications constantly at all hours of the day. We send cunning emojis to people we know the moment they cross our minds, just because they crossed our minds. The virtual world has become our world.

The virtual world is like an imagined world that is instantly and always accessible to us. Imagination, though, is about possibility, and possibility beckons to tomorrow. Since the tendency is to keep Blackness contained in a tomorrowless state, unsurprisingly, history has nothing to say about the imaginative capacity of Black folks. But the imaginations of Black cowboys still persist. Their impossible returns still beckon. Indeed, our main media apparatus remains the same as Black cowboys'. Everything we access today that seems so much more real and vital than a century ago, when we were up against the physical world, from our social media to our yoga apps, is done with the same baseline medium: text. Without getting too lost in the weeds of Derridean deconstruction and poststructuralist semiotics, text today can still be understood as a system of signs that emit and resist meaning at the same time. So, what if we think of cattle brands of Black cowboys and ranchers *as* text? This is fitting since Blackness itself is the sign of opacity that does precisely this: signifies and obscures. What if then, instead of only imagining these marks as text, we literally reimagine these marks *into* text? What if instead of the usual, conventional text gracing our screens, we had the very marks that these forgotten engineers of the cattle trail invented as expressions of their own impossible returns? As marks of identity, of mastery and expertise, of acumen. Of presence. To usher these designs back into everyday life, bypassing the abyss of over a century of forgetting, to land them into our technological future, would be nothing short of an impossible return. And, certainly, the return would be impossible.

In what could be seen as this book's parent or grandparent, or maybe cousin or (evil?) stepsister, *My Works, Ye Mighty* by Christian Bök (my predecessor as writer in residence at Athabasca University), the notion of Derrida's mark is referenced as one of the endless chain of meaning-makers that Bök guides us through. From Derrida to Borges, Bök questions what the basic element of meaning is. For Borges, at the far end of the scale, it was the archive of all archives. For Derrida, it was simply the mark. For Derrida, though, the mark was as elusive as it was meaningful. Many scholars have reconsidered his notion of the mark in terms of race. Most meaningful to me are Stuart Hall, for whom race is the mark of difference and acts as a signifier without fixed meaning; Henry Louis Gates, Jr., for whom Blackness is a rhetorical mark within

Western discourse; and many others for whom deconstruction and poststructuralist approaches are elucidated and challenged by concepts of race and Blackness in particular.[35] Truly, though, many of those scholars do not sit neatly on either side of the elucidation/challenge divide, but incorporate and involve both. Palimpsestic Blackness, which in my formulating could certainly be understood similarly, is re-covered through the marks of Black cattle brands. The mark (and language in general) creates meaning and resists meaning; it gestures beyond itself but refers only to itself. Because palimpsestic Blackness was imposed on us, I would like to return the favour by gifting everyone with a font that is created from the marks of Black cowboys. In this way, the resisting meanings of those brands will invest everyday texts with the history of forgotten cowboys. At the same time, the secret language of our cattle brands is always bound by the Double Yoke. The resistant sign cannot *mean* clearly and that, too, is what will be invested in your everyday texts. In this sense, my Black cowboys will be returned, but what exactly can be returned when the mark itself is so unsettled? I suppose, only impossibility.

---

35 For elucidation, see Fred Moten, *In the Break: The Aesthetics Of The Black Radical Tradition* (Minneapolis: University of Minnesota Press, 2003) and Christina Sharpe, *In the Wake: On Blackness and Being* (Durham, NC: Duke University Press, 2016); for how concepts of race are challenged, see among others Sylvia Wynter, *On Being Human as Praxis* (Durham, NC: Duke University Press, 2015), bell hooks, *Black Looks: Race and Representation* 2 ed. (New York: Routledge, 2015), and Katherine McKittrick, *Demonic Grounds: Black Women and the Cartographies of Struggle* (Durham, NC: Duke University Press, 2006).

THE FONT OF PALIMPSESTIC BLACKNESS

My pathway was clear: I would return the designs of Black cowboys to the technological future by creating a font that was directly based on their cattle brands. In many cases, this would be straightforward. After all, a lot of brands are simply letters. Take Benjamin Washington, for example. Though his parents were American, Washington was born in the U.K. in roughly 1876 (his D.O.B. ranges in documents from 1874–77). Very little is known of his early life, other than it contains so much tantalizing possibility. How and why did his parents make the journey to the U.K.? Had either of them ever been enslaved at some point? (The name Washington was popularly chosen by formerly enslaved Africans, though not exclusively.) Like so much of Black history, and as we saw with the poetic stratigraphy of John Ware's brand, the answers to these questions are mainly captive to the *unknown*. What is certainly known is that Washington emigrated to Canada as a young man, and, after stops in Winnipeg and Edmonton, settled himself in Northern Alberta, near the town of Grouard, where he homesteaded for a number of years and kept a small ranch. In 1915, he registered a cattle brand in his name. Here it is:

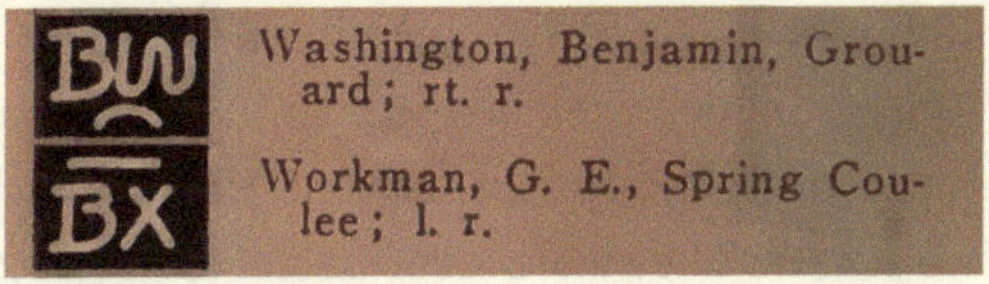
Washington, Benjamin, Grouard; rt. r.

Workman, G. E., Spring Coulee; l. r.

FIG 8 Benjamin Washington Cattle Brand.

If the most basic brand *mark* is a simple bar produced by a running iron, then it might be said that a brand consisting of simple initials is the most basic brand. To the extent that brands are identifying marks, that is, they identify ownership, initials do so by placing identity first. This basic mode of brand expression is akin to the boom of eponymous stylings of designers that emerged in the eighties when I was a teenager. *Polo* wasn't just *Polo*; it was *Polo* by Ralph Lauren. Equally, the labels that dominated our fashion landscape were sought-after (or we perceived them to be sought-after) because of the names they stood for: Calvin Klein, Liz Claiborne, or Perry Ellis were familiar and prominent identifiers that now stood alongside common, enduring ones like Coca-Cola and Levi's. Some of these names were so ubiquitous, so deeply entrenched in the general zeitgeist that they literally became singular. In fashion and luxury Versace, Armani, and Gucci joined Prince, Sting, and Madonna as one-name wonders on the music side of things. In many cases, their logos were even further whittled down to single initials, like Fendi's "FF," Gucci's "G," or Dolce and Gabbana's "D&G." This trend somewhat continues today with multinational banks like BMO (Bank of Montreal) and RBC (Royal Bank of Canada), restaurants like KFC (Kentucky Fried Chicken), and product/retail brands like PC (President's Choice) and, of course, HBC (Hudson's Bay Company), whose original names are rarely said and, maybe, scarcely remembered.

These stylings, which were just seen as marketing moves from the business perspective, worked because they directly invoked identity in two senses. They were identifiable, as in recognizable, in an unadorned, unobstructed way; equally, they were identifiable in the sense that they seemed to represent the most simplistic rendering of the brand, implying some level of unimpeded access to that elusive, inherent quality that we all yearned to engage, that we all sought to identify ourselves with. This, too, I see in the marks of Black cowboys who registered their initials as their brand. In the case of Benjamin Washington there is an added layer akin to the singularity of names like Prince or Seal. Normally, when I identify a Black cowboy or rancher's brand, I first encounter their Blackness in some archived document. For example, I might come across their name in a census where their racial status is declared, often with a scribbled out or a palimpsestic *B*, for Black, written crossly over a presumed or prewritten *W*, for white. This kind of "overwriting" is very common in censuses when it comes to identifying Black residents. It's as though the enumerator is so predisposed to anticipating anything but a Black person that they instinctively write something else in advance before being compelled to change their entry. I've hardly noticed it for any other racial designation (but to be perfectly honest, I am mainly just looking for instances of Black presence, so I very well could be missing other examples). I can honestly say I've never noticed it for white people. That is, I've never seen a *W* written on top of something else. That's significant. I should point out that Canadian censuses are not always consistent about noting race. It's as though the national impairment of Colour Blindness, which so many white Canadians have traditionally viewed with pride is a delusion (I get it, what you're trying to say is that the difference in our skin colours does not have any hierarchical significance to you — but you still treat us differently and convince yourself that you're just being "normal"), as well as an impediment to those of us trying to prove Black presences exist where you assume otherwise. The understanding that these white Canadians have of colour blindness is nothing more than a systemic bias which accommodates the normalizing of whiteness and the erasure of Blackness. Imagine, for example, coming across the name "Benjamin Washington" in the census, and then seeing, like so many others listed, that he was originally from England. Why would you think anything further about his race? See what I mean? Systemic erasure masquerading as progressive "equality."

Thus, in most cases, I thrill to find the evidence of a historic Black presence first on a census. Or, if it is not first on a census, it is in scouring local histories, often from the sixties and seventies. This is during a time in which the federal government was encouraging communities in this practice in the build-up to the nation's centenary in 1967. Many rural municipalities took advantage of the occasion to produce historical accounts of their region. Some of them occasionally mentioned the single Black person, or Black couple, or Black family, or — on rare occasion — entire Black community living in their midst. This, too, like the census discoveries, is a thrilling event that I cherish, particularly (though not exclusively) when I encounter names I've never seen before. Once I discover a Black presence, either through the census or an old local history, I then go to the brand books, going back as far as makes sense for the time period of the individual I've noted. Most of the time, I find nothing. But once in a while, there it is: a cattle brand that has been languishing in the text, waiting for someone — waiting for me — to find it again. This is the greatest thrill and I've only felt it about a dozen times, so rare are these brands.

In the case of Benjamin Washington, something unusual happened. I saw his name in a brand book before I learned of his Blackness elsewhere. If you're just looking for cowboys in general, then, sure, a historic cattle and horse brand book is a fine place to look. But it is not a logical place to begin a search for Black cowboys. Race is not mentioned anywhere in books of this sort and does not have to be mentioned anywhere. It's a book on cattle brands, not a census. Even Canadian censuses, the most likely sacrament of catalogued identities, do not hallelujah their racial categories all of the time. So, brand books? But there it was: Washington, Benjamin, Grouard, AB. And I raised my eyebrow looking at it. The fact is, stereotypes aside, it is possible to consider *Washington* as the closest thing to a Black surname that we've got on this continent. In an article in February 2011, *The Atlantic* once considered, "How Washington Became the Blackest Name in America."[36] It turns out the name has the highest proportion of Black people bearing it than any other last name on this continent. A remarkable 90% of Washingtons are Black. In a sense, *Washington* is a mark for Blackness. But it might also be a mark of *choosing.* It is speculated that the name is so common to Black people because of

36 Garance Franke-Ruta, "How 'Washington' Became the Blackest Name in America," *The Atlantic*, 21 February 2011, https://www.theatlantic.com/politics/archive/2011/02/how-washington-became-the-blackest-name-in-america/71511/.

the renaming process Africans were subjected to through slavery. We were deprived of our indigenous ethnic names. We had slave names forced on us. Sometimes, like brand marks, those names were reflections of the enslavers' identities. But just as often, these names represented choices.

Enslaved Africans mostly had no surnames and so came by them variously. Many of them did not wait for slavery to be abolished, but used names that were circulated among them as a form of community. Some chose to use an enslaver's name because it connected them – as far back as they could remember – to an ancestor, a gesture of lineage and continuity amid the tumult imposed by slavery. Some simply improvised their choices. In the famous account of his life *Up from Slavery*, Booker T. Washington admits that he simply invented his last name spontaneously when attendance was being called at school. Up to that point, he had only ever been known singularly by "Booker."[37] It is not known for certain why *Washington* is prevalent among Black people, but the speculation is that it was a name associated with freedom: though George Washington owned slaves, by the middle of the nineteenth century, it was common knowledge that his will instructed their release from bondage. Though we don't know for certain, it is possible that many formerly enslaved people chose *Washington* based on the idea of promised freedom. Similarly, it is speculated that names like Jefferson and Jackson were adopted as a result of being associated with the former presidents. These are names that many

---

37 Booker T. Washington, *Up from Slavery* (Oxford: Oxford University Press, 2000), 20.

of us carry to this day. Perhaps this makes *Washington* something of a luxury brand in Black history. But instead of the consumerist value of affluence that might have been sought with Gucci or Dior in the eighties, Black people in the nineteenth century were exercising a powerful agency and *choosing* the brand of freedom. Over 163,000 of us carry Washington, making it the most commonly Black name in America. I didn't know this statistic when I spotted the name in the *Alberta Horse and Cattle Brands 1915*, but I had my suspicions. Sure enough, a quick search through the indexes of various brand books for other years turned up almost no other Washingtons. For a common enough sounding name, it is vanishingly uncommon on the cattle-driving Canadian prairies.

Strangely, I didn't do anything further. Not right away. I didn't go to a census or try to locate a local history for the town of Grouard. It's as though I didn't trust my own instinct. Or, rather, I didn't want to be disappointed by my own instinct. In some ways, this enterprise – chasing down Black brands while reassessing how to locate my African Blackness on the Prairie – felt like its own impossible return. Relying on my instinct to uncover Black presences in history did feel like a recovery, but, as I've already pointed out, recovery itself can feel like a *re-covering*, especially if you've been raised here, this place that constantly denies your instincts about your place here (remember my Dunning–Kruger police, Officer B.?). I had my suspicions about the name Washington, but in some ways the very feeling of suspicion created doubts that were actually triggering. This may not make sense to you at first but bear with me: being raised by my biological immigrant parents came with its confusions; however, being raised by my adoptive parental province was downright disorienting. I remember once complaining to my parents about receiving racist abuse from "playful" kids at the park. My mother, in her immigrant, 1970s, pseudo-Black-power perspective, advised me to tell those kids that "Black is beautiful," the next time it happened again. Duly — because it always happened — when the next time came, I retorted with my mother's magic words and waited for the spell to take effect. Honestly, the words sounded meaningless to me. After all, these kids were taunting me with the N-word and other abuses precisely because Black was *not* seen as beautiful. I didn't understand the power of *counter*-assertion that Black leaders like Huey P. Newton and Malcolm X had been performing through the late sixties, nor how powerfully such discourse may have affected my parents, who had immigrated from a country where Black *was* beautiful by default and who were learning the hard way that countries like Canada, where Black was not in the majority, begged to differ. I just wanted the solution to my immediate problem. I wanted the racist noise to stop. I wanted some special sorcery to knock those words out of their mouths, to twist their tongues into silence, to truly shut them up. It just didn't seem to me that "Black is beautiful" was going to achieve anything. What happened was that my abuser was as confused by those words as I was. As I stood there, feigning defiance, hoping beyond hope that there was something more to the words, something secret that I couldn't see, that would invoke the spell I was after, he, too, stood there in bafflement. We both stood, staring at each other, uncomprehending, unsure of what I had unleashed, trying to pierce its nonsensical mystery. Eventually, he shrugged and left. And that was that. I didn't know what had happened. The words seemed to have worked, though I could see plainly that they had not worked. All that their juju had revealed was that if you placed the world of my parents' beautiful Blackness next to the world of my taunter's suspicious whiteness, I lived more in the world of the taunters I faced; my perceptions were more aligned with their perceptions. In facing them, I could not help but see something of myself.

This sharing burdened me in later life. The burden became something of who I am. Triggers drew me back to decisive moments like my mirrored taunter, causing indecision in my adult life. Seeing the name Washington raised suspicions in me about his potential Blackness. But raising suspicions also raised the spectre of that suspicious mirror from my past. I couldn't feel the suspicion and react triumphantly, chase down Washington's Blackness, and exult. My first instinct was to hesitate over an unconscious and unresolved guilt. I actually looked at that brand several times before I finally chose to act on my hunch. I eventually forced myself to look through censuses around the period of the year the brand was registered (1915). I know my trepidation sounds irrational. But I grew up in Truman's version of Alberta. Although I remind myself regularly that truest history is the multi-voiced one, and that multiple voices have been silenced throughout Prairie history, I still instinctively anticipate the authority of absented Blackness. And that is not a good feeling: to be confirmed in the consciousness of an already misinformed public imagination as a nonentity, that you really don't belong here, that no Black person does, that there is no history of Black people here and so you don't deserve a tomorrow, that Black presence is an oxymoron. The tragedy is, this is my default. So I didn't want to look up Benjamin Washington in a census because my instinct was that – despite the legitimate sign of his name – he would not be Black. I did not want to feel that disappointment. Again.

But I didn't. Benjamin Washington turns up in a number of censuses. I found him, first, in the 1921 census, living in the Peace River district, and in the column called "Racial or Tribal Origin," the word "Negro" is scrawled over top of what looks like an initial attempt to write something else. There it was: his palimpsestic Blackness in evidence. I was thrilled. But there were some quirks, an inevitability you encounter when you wade through the mire of censuses on a regular basis. His parents are noted as being English. Maybe this is true, but in other censuses he reports them as being American. Anomalies of this kind would need addressing, but now that I had confirmed Washington's Blackness, I allowed myself to explore his cattle brand first. Benjamin Washington's brand presents his initials on top of an inverted quarter circle, as though poised at a podium or on a stage or something like that.

Brands that have this feature (the inverted circle below the letters) strike me as raising or elevating the letters of their brand. There is another version of this feature that is standard. It occurs when the circle is flipped around the other way and the letters above are nestled in base of the curve, physically connected to it. This brand is called a "rocking" brand because it gives the impression that the letters are placed on a rocker (the quarter circle). Was this Benjamin Washington's way of attempting to raise himself above the fray, to lift himself, to stand out in his community? There was a common discourse among Black communities that involved "uplift," a movement around racial solidarity, upward mobility, religious propriety, and, controversially, respectability. In fact, it was a somewhat divisive concept among Black folks (especially with regard to respectability), but the discourse was especially popular during the late nineteenth and early twentieth centuries. This is a period that coincides with Washington's ranching activities and the registration of his brand. Might his rising quarter circle encompass a gesture toward that contemporaneous Black discourse around uplift?

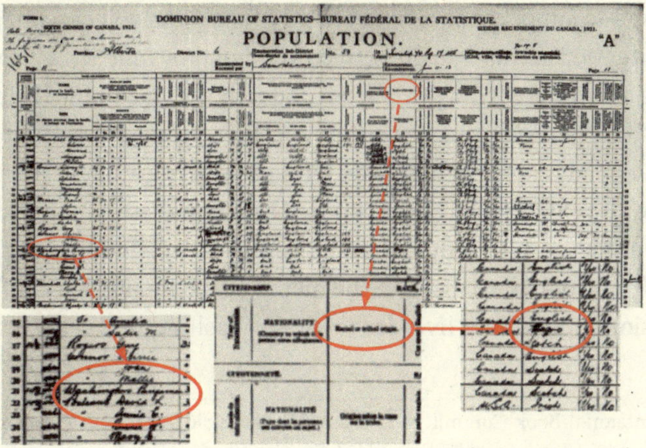

FIG 9 Benjamin Washington's Palimpsestic Blackness (1921 Federal Census).

I later located Washington in a local history called *Pioneers who Blazed the Trails*, which focuses on the High Prairie region in Northern Alberta. He is described as a singular Black man who was held in deep respect by his community. His mention as "the only negro to ever farm in this district" and "the only negro in Grouard" is completely consistent with other representations of Black people (especially men) and is so prevalent as to represent a trope.[38] But there are some unresolved gaps in Washington's story that mark the representation of his identity in cattle brands. Washington appears to have been involved in the British Home Children project. This project has a history that is deep and complex and is beyond the scope of my discussion here. The British Home Children project was a program for children who had been orphaned, often in London. They were raised to be labourers and were sent to Australia and Canada to support the work of family farms. As you can imagine, the situation seems fraught with power dynamics and the valuation of human life according to labour productivity. One cannot help but note how perilously close this arrangement comes to similar contexts already explored in this text. Indeed, there are many stories of abuse and exploitation of the children sent into these circumstances. One might certainly question the degree to which most of these children would have been at the mercy of the institutions making decisions about their lives for them. In Washington's case, several

38 Centennial Book Committee F.W.U.A. High Prairie Local 204, *Pioneers Who Blazed the Trail: Local History of High Prairie, Alberta* (High Prairie, AB: Centennial Book Committee F.W.U.A. High Prairie Local 204, 1968), 80; 158.

censuses suggest he may not have even been literate, which raises more questions about the education he was provided and the additional vulnerability such a circumstance would have placed him in. Regardless, Benjamin Washington was sent to a well-known farm in Russell, Manitoba: the Barnardo Industrial Farm. He arrived there in 1892 and by 1901 he was in Edmonton, Alberta. Nothing is known of his life at the industrial farm or his journey to Alberta, just as nothing is known of his early life in London. His parenthood is unclear. In one source, he is identified as an American who moved to the U.K. But in most of the archived materials, England is noted as his birthplace. His involvement in the industrial training farm in Russell, MB links him to the British charity organization Barnardo's, which was established in the 1860s and is an entity that still exists today. This corroborates my suspicion that he was likely an orphan or came from family straits so severe that he was unable to be properly cared for. How well connected to his parents was he? He lists his own birthday variously in different documents, though the year is consistently between 1874 and 1877. Sometimes the date is May 1; sometimes it is March 1, or March 12, or February 12. He also appears to have had siblings, a brother and a sister; however, they don't appear to have participated in the same agricultural training scheme as he did, and so far I have been unable to locate them in the archives. In short, it is very hard to know who Benjamin Washington was prior to arriving in Canada.

One thing, therefore, that stands out starkly to me is his cattle brand. Washington occupied himself in a number of ways after settling in Canada. He worked on freights. He was a domestic helper.

He farmed. Primarily, though, he farmed, and this is most appropriate because he was trained on an industrial farm and may have even been introduced to ranching. But farming was, ostensibly, the main purpose for which he was sent to Canada. So he wasn't a cowboy. In 1905, the year John Ware died, Washington settled in the High Prairie region in Northern Alberta. The cowboy era in Southern Alberta was sounding its death knell. By 1912, the Calgary Stampede was launched in part as a commemorative festival, a ceremony of a skillset that was anticipating its own nostalgia. Perhaps there were still traditional cowboys around when Washington

FIG 10 Close-up of Benjamin Washington's Mark (1915).

FIG 11 Benjamin Washington/Bertrand Bickersteth Historic Collaboration.

FIG 12 "B" & "W": Black Cowboy Font (2025).

registered his brand in 1915, but the lifestyle was coming to a close. It makes me wonder how much of the cowboying life he knew personally. Was he drawn to it? After all, when he arrived in Canada in 1892, the mythology of the West — its mythic frontier, its aspirations of individualism and freedom — was in full force. Did any of it infatuate him? Impossible to know. What is known is that, despite having very little practical experience of ranching, and despite not possessing any significant numbers of cattle (as per the censuses), and despite possibly not even knowing how to read or write, he imagined, designed, and registered a brand that was published only once. Subsequent years of the brand book do not contain his brand. It was as though he literally just wanted to make his mark.

I also want to mention that if he was out to make a name for himself, then this was just part of a strategy for successfully earning a living. It costs money to register a brand; you don't just do it to launch your name into orbit and escape the gravity well of anonymity. Sadly, he may simply not have been successful in this area. After all, his farming doesn't seem to have amounted to much. Eventually, he gave it up and rented the land out to other farmers while he lived on a small portion of it.[39] So, the cattle brand may have been as much a pathway to economic security as it was a shot in the dark of a different kind: the kind that bursts into light, like fireworks, dazzling against a firmament of forgotten Blackness.

---

39 High Prairie & Area History Book Society, *Trails We Blazed Together: History of Grouard, High Prairie & Surrounding Areas* (High Prairie, AB: High Prairie & Area History Book Society, 1997), 1432.

THE FONT OF IMPOSSIBLE CHOOSINGS

Perhaps Benjamin Washington was illiterate, or perhaps he was only illiterate in certain languages, like the languages that made his *choosings* impossible. Perhaps, the language of cattle brands simply allowed him to return from that impossible choosing. The language of Black cattle brands always courts the impossible return. We can see versions of this courting in another brand too. Frederick Hall was not a cowboy, but he was a horseman. He came from a farming family in Iowa in the early 1900s, helping to deliver another farmer's goods from Des Moines by rail. In Alberta, he worked at several farms and ranches in and around the Innisfail area. In 1907, he was issued a patent for his own homestead near Pine Lake. Although he noted on his application that he had no stock (only horses), he registered a brand on three different occasions.

In 1915, he registered an upward-facing quarter circle over a lazy F H. This brand can be seen as a variation of Benjamin Washington's initials. The quarter circle is positioned differently, and one of the initials is lazy instead of upright. But we can think of it as accomplishing something very similar: the simple act of leaving his mark, asserting his identity as directly as possible. In the Department of Agriculture's *Alberta Horse and Cattle Brands, 1919–20*, this same brand shows up again, as if it were an affirmation. But something interesting happens in between these two brand books. In the brand book for 1916–18, Hall's cattle brand is not present, but he registered a brand for his horses. This brand is different from his usual cattle brand. It presents his initials with three clear changes, two of them striking: both letters are now upright, the quarter circle above has been replaced by a bar below, and the *H* is gone, now substituted with a *D*. The effect is to emphasize the initials in a way that is completely different from his cattle brand. Both letters are upright; there is no ornamentation or manipulation (that is, they are not reversed or lazy or upside down) of any kind; and they are effectively underlined by the bar. It is as clear an assertion of his initials as is possible.

But I am particularly struck by the replacement of the *H* with the *D*. In one way, it makes sense to do this. Hall already had a cattle brand he had registered in the previous edition of the brand book. What's more, its purpose was different in that it was meant for cattle, whereas this one was meant for horses. Changing the initials further emphasizes the distinction: "F H" for cattle, "F D" for horses. In another view, however, the poetic one, offering different initials is like offering different identities of the same person. So who was FH compared to FD, and why choose *D* anyway? Frederick Hall's full name was Frederick Douglas Hall. If that

FIG 13 Fred Hall Brands, from top to bottom: "Quarter Circle Lazy FH" (1915 cattle); "FD Bar" (1916–18 horse); "Quarter Circle Lazy FH" (1919 cattle).

doesn't ring familiar to you at this point, it should. Though the spelling is different, the name evokes the great nineteenth-century orator and abolitionist Frederick Douglass. As I've pointed out earlier, Douglass was arguably the most famous Black person of the nineteenth century. He was a symbol of Black achievement, Black freedom, and Black agency positioned against a restrictive white society that regularly curtailed or denied the possibility of these things. His name was legendary among Black people. It would have been impossible for those two names, Frederick and Douglas/s, to be coupled and *not* to evoke the renown of the great orator.

By the time Frederick Hall was born in 1867, Frederick Douglass was already a famous man, whose autobiography was a bestseller in the U.S. *and* the U.K. It is a special kind of choosing that incorporates the most famous abolitionist of the day into the name of one of your children, particularly if you yourself had been or knew people who had been enslaved. Then, for Hall to insert it in the years between his cattle brand registration represents yet another special type of choosing. He is, in a sense, using the cattle brands as a performance of his multi-dimensioned self. The part of his identity that is associated with Frederick Douglass – the "F D Bar" brand – pops up like a middle name itself, subtle but essential. With the exception of censuses, in most of the documents that Hall identifies himself, he includes his middle name as well. It's an aspect to his identity that, frankly, most white Canadians would have been insensible to. It was an acknowledgement of his identity with a particular historical ring. Similarly, his horse brand, nestled as it was between the two publications of his cattle brand, expressed a dimensionality that would largely have gone unrecognized. This was Fred Hall nodding to his "Douglassness," nodding, that is, to his Black agency, even out here in the so-called middle of nowhere. This classic middle-of-nowhere nod (*you* know what I'm talking about), that filled me with ambivalence as a teenager, creates an entirely different response in me now.[40] Today, it allows me an impossible return, a special choosing; I see Fred Hall's middle-of-nowhere nod and I nod back.

THE FONT OF IMPOSSIBLE FREEDOM

It is a curiosity that Sierra Leone is one of the very few African countries whose name is neither African nor in an "official," colonial language. *Sierra Leone* is Portuguese but was never a colony of Portugal. The name nods to its so-called European "discoverer." Need I have said European? After all, aren't all discoverers of this nature European? The term might be redundant: European discoverer. In this same manner, the name South Africa is redundant. But South Africa is an English name, or, at least, uses English to express its name. Sierra Leone's name is an imposition invented by the naming power of Europe that sought to reconfigure Africa into an entity that suited its social and economic ambitions (for itself), essentially deeming the entire continent empty of history. Hence, Pedro de Sintra, the Portuguese navigator who "first" set eyes

40 Wink-wink.

on Sierra Leone's mountainous coastline, was reminded of lions seated on their haunches and bestowed our name upon us. Unlike many African countries that chose to reshape themselves during the period of decolonization that took place during the twentieth century, Sierra Leone did not change its name. Gold Coast became Ghana; Rhodesia became Zimbabwe. The Democratic Republic of Congo took renaming to the extreme: after independence in 1960, it became the Republic of Congo, then Zaire and finally in 1997, the Democratic Republic of Congo). And so on. But Sierra Leone stayed Sierra Leone. The English colonial governor packed up and left; English remained our official language, and it still is; and though we have no official ties to Portugal, our Portuguese name stayed Portuguese. And, despite this odd quirk of history, there is something fulfilling in the retention of this name: it too represents a form of renaming. It, too, represents an impossible choosing.

After my ancestors achieved their impossible return back across the Middle Passage, backwards through the Door of No Return, they discovered what all impossible returnees learn, what *all* returnees learn: return is impossible. They were back, but they were impossibly back, and as such they carried their "impossibleness" with them. As I showed earlier, one example of this is seen in the poetry of the Krio language itself, both structurally rooted in English and inherently expressively African. *A de kam* is itself an expression of this impossible contradiction in its refusal to speak of leaving. But after a few generations of being settled, the Krio people (who were called "Creole" throughout the nineteenth century) began to chafe at their historic connections to slavery. They rejected being identified as "former slaves" or "recaptives" and criticized the view that sought to mark them indelibly with this context. They asserted themselves as free Africans with connections to a continent whose actual histories transcended by far the single, cataclysmic intervention of the slave trade. In the 1870s, they went through a version of the Black Arts movement almost a century before Sonya Sanchez or Amiri Baraka spit any poems, or Archie Shepp blasted his Black Arts notes, or before, even, the existence of the Black Panthers. This was the period in which the somewhat pejorative term "Afro-Saxons" was applied against them, yet they were busy immersing themselves in the Africanness of their identity. They established "African" clubs. They denounced Victorian clothing (which was very commonly worn then). They championed African music. They asserted African names over their European ones. I found a reference in the *Sierra Leone Weekly News* to an Aaron Bickersteth who had taken on a Yoruba name and asserted it beside his European one. This was possibly the most consistent and, arguably, the most impactful practice of their resistance to a historical identity that flattened them into the single dimension of slavery. Actually, the legacy of ambivalent naming practices carries on among the Krio, sometimes demonstrable within a single family dynamic. I, for example, got a European name, while my sister was given an African one.

Naming is a powerful assertion of identity and, equally, can be a powerful subversion of imposed identity. I pointed out that when I first spotted the name Washington in a brand book, though I hesitated to react right away, I immediately sensed I had stumbled across a Black presence, such is the power of certain historical namings, certain impossible returns. I had a similar experience with another name I came across in a brand book, but this time, my reaction was completely different. Sensing I had come across another unremembered record of a Black presence, I immediately searched it out in the censuses corresponding to the brand book's time period. In this case, I was right. There it was in the census on my first try: Racial or tribal origin: negro. The name was Freeman. I want to point out that there are actually a number of Freemans in the Brand Books.

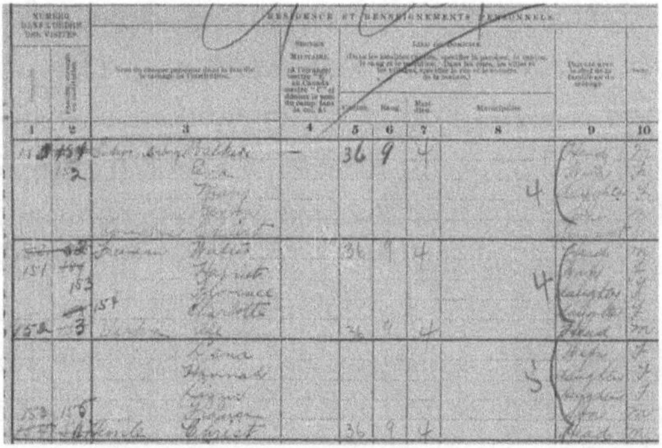

When I went to the censuses, what I did was search for any Freeman in Alberta and filtered it through racial origin. Walter Freeman's family was the only result that came back. So, while my experience made it look like every Freeman equals a Black presence, it just so happens that the first one I came across in the brand book was exactly what I was looking for.

FIG 14 The Freeman Family (Prairie Census, 1916).
FIG 15 Freeman Family's Palimpsestic Blackness.

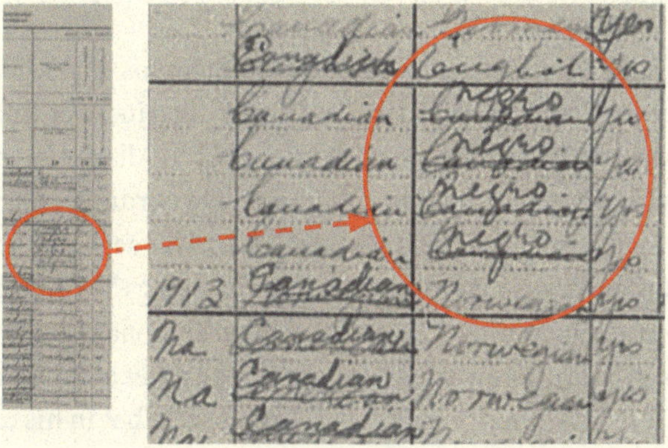

This census entry is notable for, once again, demonstrating that palimpsestic Blackness that seems almost inevitable in these early cases. Perhaps, this time, it was precisely the uncertainty of the category that caused the bureaucratic double-take. The enumerator had written "Canadian" at first (which in all contexts is the actual correct answer here) but then crossed it out and wrote "negro" over it. Perhaps he felt that doubt, which I am positing as deeply Canadian, that sensibility which understands itself to be free of "American race prejudice" and would *never* judge someone inferior on the basis of their skin colour, but *would* instinctively question how anyone who wasn't white could still constitute being Canadian in the same manner that they as white people understood themselves to be Canadian. The result is a prevaricating statistical entry ("Canadian") that exits at the same time it is entered. The result for me, though, prevarication, palimpsest, and all, is a successfully identified Black presence on the historical landscape of the Prairies. In my eyes, that is a remarkable uncovering.

Isaac Walter Freeman is as remarkable for his embodied Black presence on the Prairies as for the utter ordinariness of the life he led in Alberta. Walter moved with his family to Alberta in the early 1900s with his wife and two daughters. This ordinary fact alone makes them somewhat remarkable. Historical accounts of Black people on the Prairies seem so bent on identifying the singularity of, largely, Black men, that it is practically revolutionary to be able to point to an entire family who never graced the pages of a history book. John Ware shares this "remarkable" feat as well, but in his case it is baffling and somewhat bipolar. Despite being regularly represented as a unique figure, singular in Alberta's history as a Black cowboy, there is, at the same time, ample documented and readily available evidence of the family he married into and the family he created with his wife, Mildred. My focus is on the language of cattle brands here, so I will only digress long enough to point out that Mildred came from a large family, the Lewises, who also moved to Alberta en masse. In fact, they joined what must surely be thought of as a community of Black people. Though not as thickly populated as those in the plantation South, or those beginning to emerge westward across the United States in the wake of the abolition of slavery at the end of the Civil War, those sporadic arrivals of Black folks in Western Canada, too, constituted a protective gathering, a social network that stayed connected through church experiences, social celebrations, and labour, even when they weren't geographically next to each other.

But let me not digress much longer. I will finish this point by returning to cattle brands and pointing out that the Ware family, which consisted of six children along with John and Mildred, also proliferated several cattle brands.[41] Once again, history seems besotted with Ware's more or less single output, the Four Walking Sticks (or Four Nines) brand. I say *more or less* because it is well documented how he dropped one of the Walking Sticks from this original design fairly soon after its introduction. But the stories stop there. In fact, Ware registered several different brands. In the manner of many ranchers seeking to establish a foundational legacy, he spread the ownership of those brands throughout his family. His daughter, Nettie, and his sons, Robert and William, all had brands registered under their names in the 1900 and 1904 Brand Books.

In 1900, Nettie, the eldest child, would have been seven years old. So this was hardly an independent venture on the part of the children. John Ware was growing his business and one of the vehicles for this growth was his growing family. For me, then, it is very important to acknowledge the presence of Black families on the Prairies, particularly when they can be located in historical documents, because so much of our historical imagination has excluded the possibility of this simple, common, yet powerful dimensionality of human life. To uncover evidence of Walter Freeman, not just as an individual, but as a member of a Black family living on the historical Prairies, filled me with joy.

The Freemans lived in truly middle-of-nowhere Alberta. Walter homesteaded land near Throne, AB, which is roughly between Red Deer and the Saskatchewan border. The nearest town is Coronation, which is about 12 km northwest of Throne, along Highway 12.

---

41 Tragically, one died in infancy.

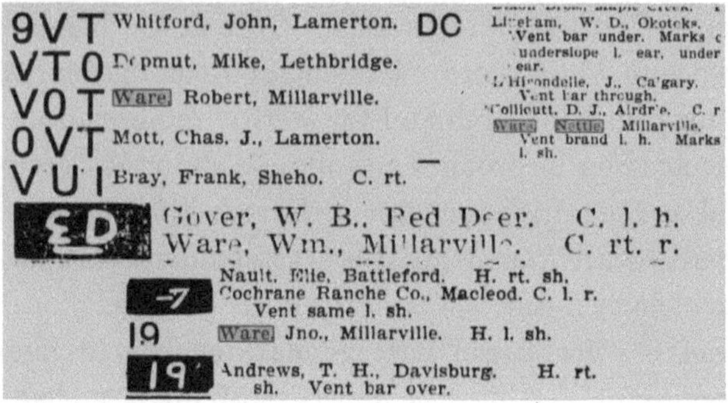
9VT Whitford, John, Lamerton.
VT0 Dempmut, Mike, Lethbridge.
V0T Ware Robert, Millarville.
0VT Mott, Chas. J., Lamerton.
VUI Bray, Frank, Sheho. C. rt.
DC Lineham, W. D., Okotoks. Vent bar under. Marks c underslope l. ear, under ear.
L'Hirondelle, J., Calgary. Vent bar through.
Collicutt, D. J., Airdrie. C. r
Ware Nettie Millarville. Vent brand l. h. Marks l. sh.
Gover, W. B., Red Deer. C. l. h.
Ware, Wm., Millarville. C. rt. r.
-7 Nault, Elie, Battleford. H. rt. sh.
Cochrane Ranche Co., Macleod. C. l. r. Vent same l. sh.
19 Ware Jno., Millarville. H. l. sh.
19 Andrews, T. H., Davisburg. H. rt. sh. Vent bar over.

The area is notable for being settled during the early part of the twentieth century, mainly 1909–15. This is precisely when Walter shows up in the documents. This, too, might show why his census enumerator's entry stammers with contradictions. Column 17, the column dedicated to "Nationality" follows the columns for "Year of Immigration to Canada" and "Year of Naturalization" (respectively, columns 15 and 16). Together, the three columns make up the "Citizenship" category. Having learned in column 13 that this Black homesteading family had all been born in Canada (Ontario) and had taken up the call to come West and earn the fruits of freedom and independence that was owed to any true-blooded Canadian (male) who is worth the salt, the enumerator struggles with the knowledge that people who, in his view, are a very "untrue-blooded Canadian" family have answered that call and are prospering as though they were as capable and worthy to do so as *he was*. That is, on seeing this Black homesteading family was entirely born and bred in Canada, he is forced to enter *absolutely nothing* in columns

---

FIG 16 Family Brands, from left to right: Robert (VOT), Nettie (DC), William (Crazy 3 D), and John Ware (19).

15 and 16: this family of Canadians (whose parents were also born and bred in Canada) never immigrated and were not naturalized but were already *naturally* Canadian. So, naturally, the enumerator's logic took over and he quite reasonably entered "Canadian." This is the usual entry for people who were born in Canada, particularly if their parents were also born in Canada. But then, paradoxically, his *Canadian* sensibilities took over and he doubted his own reasoning. I can only imagine this apparent contradiction of the eye contributed to an apparent confusion of the hand, resulting in the scrawled-over entry for the Freeman family's "racial or tribal" origin in column 18. In some ways it is fitting, though. This, in black and white bureaucratic text, is how Canada officially sees us: a collision of origins in which an unexpected Canadianness is rendered almost illegible by the superscription of an equally unexpected Blackness.

However unexpected, the Freeman's family story is one of the most Canadian stories there is, if Canadian stories involve a search for wider opportunities in the quest for self-determination. Walter Freeman moved from Ontario to find fortune in the West. He was born there in 1882 to Arlington and Liza, who were also both born in Ontario. Arlington's parents came to Canada from the U.S., and because Arlington was born in 1854 or 1855, there is some suggestion that his parents had experienced slavery on some level, though it is impossible to know exactly what that level was. There are, however, some very persuasive clues. The first clue is the timeframe: Arlington was born in Canada while slavery was still legal in the U.S. The period between 1833 – when slavery was abolished in Canada – and 1865 – when it was abolished in the U.S. – was intense with activity along the Underground Railroad. This, along with the fact that Ontario was the most common Canadian terminus of the Underground Railroad, strongly suggests his parents engineered an escape to Canada. Another clue has to do with the gaps in the family's knowledge. On his death certificate, Arlington's father is named (Robert), but his mother's maiden name is unknown. The certificate doesn't ask for a mother's first name, so we don't know if it was unknown as well. I suspect not, but, either way, the indication is that the family's history was touched on some level by slavery. This is primarily due to my third and final clue: the family name itself. Freeman. This is the very reason why I instantly suspected a Black Prairie presence when I came across this name the first time. It is why I didn't hesitate to go to the census in the manner that I hesitated with *Washington*. Indeed, it is, prima facie, why I discovered a family of *Canadian* "negroes" when I located them in the census. It is also why Arlington may not have known his mother's maiden name, whether or not he knew her first name. Freeman (or Freedman) is a name that Black people chose to celebrate the dimensionality of their humanity that had once been denied under the uncompromising imposition of slavery. It signals the possibility of choice, as well as the path to a tomorrow that was abrogated by the slave trade (initiated by the "Door of No Return") and remains dismissed in North America's resultant Blackness (being viewed as fundamentally ahistorical). It is the reflection of a humanity that they always knew they had but were not allowed to acknowledge. Yes, they often chose it, and so it was a *choosing*, but it was also not a choice at all; it was a necessary declaration; it was a ground zero assertion of fact;

it was a return to who they had always been. They had performed their own reverse journey through the Door of No Return, just like the Krio of Sierra Leone. The name "Freeman" was a powerful act of reclamation, the choosing of their own impossible return.

This, I suspect, is why I didn't hesitate when I saw the name, as I did with *Washington*. In the case of *Washington*, the aura of slavery mysteriously, inevitably emanates. Its presence can – and often is – rejected, but the aura haunts. "Freeman" seems to do something completely different. It inaugurates; it births. Think of Leonard Pitts Jr.'s evocation of the name in his Pulitzer-Prize winning novel *Freeman*, in which a newly emancipated Black man called Sam Freeman learns to rethink who he is within the context of gained liberty. Think, too, of Baby Suggs in Toni Morrison's *Beloved*. In a famous passage where she gains her freedom, she delivers a sermon in the clearing and the new relationship that freedom confers between Blackness and the Black body.

> "Here," she said, "in this here place, we flesh; flesh that weeps, laughs; flesh that dances on bare feet in grass. Love it. Love it hard. Yonder they do not love your flesh. They despise it. They don't love your eyes; they'd just as soon pick em out. No more do they love the skin on your back. Love your hands! Love them. Raise them up and kiss them. Touch others with them, pat them together, stroke them on your face 'cause they don't love that either."[42]

---

42 Toni Morrison, *Beloved* (New York: Alfred A. Knopf, 2021), 88.

Washington was a name that may have been imposed and that may have been chosen, but *Freeman* signals choice. It, too, may have been imposed and may have been chosen, but the poetry for me is in the evocation of what is being chosen. It is the renewal of dimensions, the renewal to love.

This is the central Canadianness of Freeman's family story. They wanted a better life and their Canadian lives allowed them to pursue that essential thing that defined them in the most authentic way possible, even when Canada itself stood in their way. This is no different than it is for McDonalds, Riels, Chans, Romanoffs, or Nenshis. For many of the families who came to this country through the Underground Railroad, the initial realization of freedom was quickly tempered by the realities of racism that existed here, too. But the benefits on offer for other groups were apprehensible to them too. So, despite resistance, they formed communities; they established networks; some of them started businesses; many of them worked land they had acquired; some of them answered the call to go West and help build the nation. This, too, is an essential part of the Canadian story, which we can never ignore is very much enmeshed in territorial claims. Black aspirants were enmeshed in this history too, though, as people whose humanity had been flattened in stark, imposed relationship to the land, the dynamics of their particular enmeshment are not straightforward. Arlington and his wife Eliza had seven sons. The third son, Walter, chose to answer the call and go West, seeking that sense of independent achievement, individual autonomy, that ownership and industry that for many settlers in that day *was* freedom. In coming to middle-of-nowhere Alberta with his family, Walter was simply seeking to return to his name.

His family had been farmers in Ontario. His father had owned a mixed farming operation since he was twenty years old and Walter continued this tradition in Throne. He homesteaded land that eventually produced crops and he raised cattle as well. One of the few documents I found of Walter, other than census or homesteading documents, is a brief mention in the newspaper of Walter buying a Hereford bull for $200 in 1918. It is a small note, but a large confirmation of his status as a cattle man. The other confirmation is, of course, his published literary works graced in the pages of cattle brand books. The "Quarter Circle Reverse F Four" brand does something slightly different than Benjamin Washington's "B W" or Frederick Hall's "F D" brands.

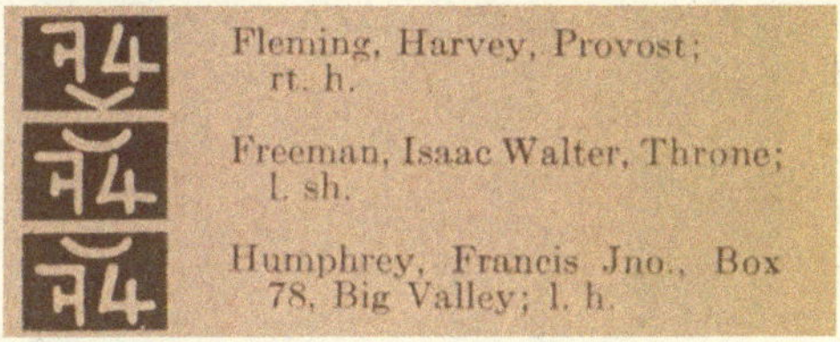
Fleming, Harvey, Provost; rt. h.

Freeman, Isaac Walter, Throne; l. sh.

Humphrey, Francis Jno., Box 78, Big Valley; l. h.

While those brands focused on the intrinsic simplicity of initials – that is, they presented the straightforward letters as a straightforward representation of who they were, unembellished – Walter Freeman's brand does the opposite. The *F* of this brand is emphasized, it is reversed, it is all embellishment. It is as though it was urging us to look at the *F*, if nothing else.

FIG 17 Walter Freeman's "Quarter Circle Reverse F Four" Brand.

It signals the singular importance of the letter because, in this case, singularity signifies dimensionality. The *F* has to be noticed because it is the F of freedom. It is the freedom one family reclaimed when they returned to their rightful name.

PART 5

THE IMPOSSIBLE RETURN

THE IMPOSSIBLE BICKERSTETH

Some names are more rightful than others. Some names return in the most unexpected ways. One of my obsessions has been to determine who the first Bickersteth was. By this, I mean, of course, the first *African* Bickersteth. My curiosity is prompted by one of the unusual historical legacies I claim through my Krio background. In Sierra Leone, Krio ethnicity is distinguished from the other indigenous ethnicities by our collision with the West. We are marked by it and we pass on that mark like an indelible scar that is rebirthed again and again. We are Christians. Our language is hybridized. We were known once as Afro-Saxons. And we have European last names. As you know, this last fact is partially due to slavery's merciless mortar expunging our original, African names and grinding us out with European ones, sometimes imposed, sometimes chosen. We are impossible returnees. But there is another wrinkle to that story that does not follow the same path across the Middle Passage in the same way. In fact, that path was quite literally disrupted.

After Sierra Leone was established as an African colony in Africa, it went through a number of status transformations. At first, it was nothing at all that could be identified as an official people in the modern or Western sense: it was simply a settlement administered by the Sierra Leone Company, which had been run by a number of abolitionists in England. Then in 1808, it was made a British Crown Colony. These were rocky times for the colonists, as well as for the conception of the colony itself. Although they had returned as free people to establish a new beginning in a town they duly called Freetown, slavery itself still abounded. In fact, it still surrounded them. For all of its history connected to the abolition movement of the eighteenth century, Sierra Leone remained a central site for slavery well into the nineteenth century. The Sierra Leone Company had been run privately and was often struggling with finances and organizational cohesion. In 1807, Britain abolished the slave trade. But don't get too excited. Yes, this move was an important one and signalled a moral shift in Britain's policies, but it was just as much brought about by economic incentives, as well as strategic foreign policy moves. Just in case you missed this detail, it wasn't slavery itself that was abolished; it was the slave trade. That meant that British citizens could still legally own slaves, that Africans would still legally remain flattened non-humans without full rights. But it meant that the buying and selling of Africans (or anyone) was no longer legal, and it did open the door to conferring some new rights to them, as well as creating the path that eventually would lead to total abolition of slavery. But at this point, slavery itself was still legal. I should also point out that Britain's abolition of the slave trade, important as it was, was only applicable to Britain, and several other countries still regularly engaged in trading slaves.

And among slave traders, Sierra Leone remained a valued site to acquire Africans. This created a surreal situation, akin to any speculative novel, in which the colony of returned Africans, of free Africans, were surrounded by the tumult and energies of enslaving activities, even as they struggled to live out the freedoms of their hard-won return to Africa. Do you see how impossible returns are?

Some of Britain's motivations were economic and political, where, occasionally, morality took a back seat. Britain's economy was shifting to mechanized, mass-production and it no longer needed to generate labour through slaves as much as it had in the past. It also, quite paradoxically, became intent on positioning itself in the world as a beacon of morality, which was as much an attempt to change moral positions on slavery as it was a desire to be seen as a global influencer. None of these things had any impact, at least not immediately, on their so-called possessions in the Caribbean and the enormous wealth that was generated by the slave plantations there. Nevertheless, they positioned themselves as the police of the seas, literally placing navy ships along the coast to intercept and arrest any slave ships speeding toward the Americas with a hold full of enslaved Africans. When Sierra Leone became a Crown Colony in 1808, it was used strategically in the battle against the slave trade. Freetown became an administrative dropping-off point for any Africans recovered from a slave ship and released to freedom. One miracle is that some Africans returned, impossibly, more than once. Some of the African colonists were swept up into slavery again, intercepted en route to the Americas, and returned to African soil yet again. Another miracle is that the already hybridized Krio people became even more so, as ships that had scoured slaves from all along the western coast of Africa were returned to Freetown, and those Africans settled there, melding with the current inhabitants.

So African traditions from all over West Africa commingled and coalesced in a way that predates the cosmopolitanism of modern, immigrant nations like the U.S. and Canada today. And though these newest returnees had managed, just, to escape the enduring horrors of slavery on the other side of the Atlantic, they still underwent powerful transformations upon settling in Freetown. The colony had always been directed by British sensibilities and making it a Crown Colony in 1808 only made the cultural connections official. The governor was British. The laws of the colony were British. The colonists learned English in British schooling systems. They became Christian. They took on European names. Bickersteth was almost certainly one of those names.

Bickersteth is an unusual last name. I'm often told it sounds like a writer's name (in combination with Bertrand, I assume). It seems Dickensian. It feels literary and heavy with history at the same time. I will admit, its unusual factor made it useful for doing genealogical searches. That is how I know that it is not one of the names that recrossed the Atlantic from Nova Scotia to Sierra Leone. Besides the fact that it does not appear on any of the documentation related to the "Book of Negroes" or ship manifests of that famous flotilla, it doesn't even appear in North America until the nineteenth century. I very likely do have ancestors who came from Nova Scotia; they simply did not have the name Bickersteth, or to be more accurate, they did not *begin* with the name Bickersteth. As a child, I struggled with the name. It should have been acceptable as a European name, but it was an unusual one, and so people stumbled over it. I regularly had (and have) people unconsciously call me Bickerstaff, a variant of the same name. When I was a literature student, I was pleasantly surprised to learn that the Irish satirist Jonathan Swift had made use of the pseudonym Isaac Bickerstaff. It seemed to confer some sort of acceptability in my eyes. But for the most part, especially when I was younger, the name felt like an albatross. Coupled with Bertrand, it made for an alliterative mouthful that seemed to qualify it as foreign to my Canadian peers. In truth, I felt like an imposter. I did not feel I could authentically own the name in the way that my friends of European descent would enthusiastically point out the logical origins of "Smith," "Cooper," or "Baker," as they were so obviously attached to recognizable vocations in Europe. But Bickersteth has no such readily available relation. Though I was not one hundred percent sure at the time about the name's origins, as far as my family was concerned, I was suspicious; it seemed to have the whiff of slavery about it. It was a suspicion that had me paralyzed by my own needs: I desperately wanted it confirmed; I desperately did not want it confirmed.

As a student at the University of British Columbia, I worked at the University Press part-time. To my amazement, one of the U.K. distribution deals the press had acquired at the time was a book called *The Bickersteth Diaries*. Many people commented on this coincidence and wondered if there could possibly be any familial links between us. My reaction was embarrassment. The book seemed only to confirm my status as an imposter of the Bickersteth family name. The innocent question of could there possibly be a family connection, for me, hinged on what was buried in the presumption of the word *possibly*. Could there *possibly* be a family connection? It seemed to assert the natural order of things: Bickersteth is a European name. So what *possibilities* allowed for me, a Black presence in North America, to share this name with one of their British authors? I didn't fully know the history of Sierra Leone at that point, but I did know that however my family became connected to the name Bickersteth was almost certainly *not* the same way in which my very curious colleagues at the Press were connected to theirs. Because of my confusing Prairie upbringing, in which everything about my Blackness was both anomalous and somehow my fault, my reaction to all of this intense curiosity in my background was shame. I dodged questions. I changed the subject. I shrugged mutely. One of the editors very kindly and very innocently offered to put me in touch with Ursula, the project's family contact in England, who then sent me a very kind, very polite letter noting her awareness of some American Bickersteths in Michigan and her delight to discover some in Canada. None of her words betrayed an awareness of the *possibility* that she was corresponding with an African who shared *her* name. "I hope you'll have a good year," she wrote. "And if you felt inclined to write to me, I would be very happy to hear from you." All of these unspoken presumptions, as well as my halfling history, triggered imposter syndrome. I didn't know how to insert myself – *my* family story – into the assumptions that were being made around me. I felt shame, and still to my shame today, I left her letter unanswered.

She noted that one of her uncles had spent time in Western Canada in the early 1900s before settling in Toronto as the Warden of Hart House at U of T. He had even written a book about his pioneering days that she hoped I might find interest in, even though, she pointed out, I appeared to be in British Columbia and the book was set in rural Alberta. This surprised me. All my life, I had assumed that my small family band of Bickersteths were not only the only Bickersteths in Alberta, but that they had only ever been the *only* Bickersteths to set foot in Alberta. As far as the African Bickersteths are concerned, I was right. But here was another Bickersteth, a *real* Bickersteth, who had been there three generations earlier. Although I never responded to Ursula's letter, I took a deep interest in acquiring this book and learning more.

Burgon Bickersteth, the book's author, was an Anglican lay missionary who answered the church's call to provide ministry to new communities in the far-flung Western Canadian wilderness. It was a difficult task but appealed to the adventurist who wanted to witness a young nation in the throes of one of its growth spurts. Incredibly, Burgon may have arrived in rural Alberta at the same time as Walter Freeman, both men pursuing different embodiments of Western possibility. I have read his book many times and am struck by how vividly the urge to strike out and create one's own path of possibility shaped the tenor of the times. As well, it is striking how strongly this urge was connected to the shaping and development of the nation itself. Yet there were unspoken contradictions forced against each other in the process. Burgon admired the diversity of people who came to power the West with nothing but their determination and ambitions. Although he was English and had come on the unspoken presumption that England was the mother nation to this burgeoning Western Canadian province, he seemed nevertheless to take for granted that it was the variety of people that would most naturally realize the province's potential. Although, today, we are very used to giving warnings about the relativity of eurocentric bias that was both prevalent and de rigueur, Burgon seems to show almost none of it. He is practically blasé about the nationalities he comes into contact with. At one point in the book, after trekking through the middle-of-nowhere wilderness for hours, he comes face to face with my mirror.

> I proceeded on my way – ten miles through the bush – without seeing a soul except two negro children.... About 1 P.M. I arrived at Hilton's. Mrs. Hilton is a full-blooded negress, and keeps a "stopping place" – in other words an inn, if you can call two rather tumble-down log shacks by such a name.... Mrs. Hilton, with her shiny countenance and two rows of grinning white teeth, soon called me into the little shack, which served as kitchen, dining-room, and her bedroom, "stoppers" being put in two double beds in the other shack.[43]

My jaw nearly dropped when I read that passage, but it was all small beer for Brother Burgon. As it turns out, there was a Black colony of sorts in Northern Alberta that had only recently established itself near Campsie, and though Burgon never went

43 J. Burgon Bickersteth, *The Land of Open Doors: Being Letters from Western Canada, 1911–13* (Toronto: University of Toronto Press, 1976), 30.

directly there, I suspect he would have remained nonplussed by its presence as it was yet another manifestation of the cosmopolitan countryside he seemed to cherish.

Travelling seems to have run in the family, for Burgon's great grandfather Edward, also cherished roaming through wild territories replete with contradictory mélanges. In Edward's case though, it was the bush of West Africa that drew him. Edward Bickersteth was a missionary who, yes, went to Freetown in 1816 to help establish the Church Missionary Society there and ensure the Christian transition of the Africans who were "recaptured" from slavery. Another common thread amongst the Bickersteths is that they appear to enjoy writing about their escapades as well. In his diaries, Edward frequently mentions his jaunts through the bush, encountering new people and unexpected circumstances. While the average nineteenth-century Englishman would almost immediately upon stepping foot on the African west coast succumb to malaria or some other dread disease found only in the "dark continent," Edward seemed to be enlivened by being there. He had many plans for spreading the gospel and he set about executing them with the vigour of someone pursuing their dream job. Because he was. His dream was to prove to the world that all people had the capacity to share in the light of Christ and to continue sharing it themselves. Like many eurocentric benefactors of African projects, he connected Christian belief to the civilization of society and understood himself to be raising Africans out of barbarity.

I would like to point out that this unregulated territory of behaviours, in which Europeans traipsed across the globe, rescuing "barbarians" from their ignorance, was a version of a Wild West that would also express itself in North America. It is, in fact, the reason why most of us are unaware that there ever was such a thing as Black cowboys. The settling of the West was, too, a project of asserting civility. European settlers saw themselves as the prime administrators of vast and empty territories that needed organizing. The West was considered wild, in part, because its perceived emptiness invited this organization, but mostly it was because the emptiness of the lands was not cooperating with their plans. The inconvenience of already-present Indigenous peoples, who had their own cultural priorities, traditions, political structures, spiritual practices, family and social dynamics, personal ambitions, social aspirations, historical imagination, and narrative modalities (to name a few) hampered the settlers' vision of empty lands. Indigenous cultural priorities, etc., were therefore understood by settlers as wilful resistance (because it was) whose logical remedy was genocide (because white supremacy). The dimensionality of Indigenous peoples was met with a barbarity that named *them* barbarous, an intrusion that saw them as intruding, a lawlessness that accused them of lawlessness, a wildness that envisioned them as wild. As white people encroached on lands occupied by Indigenous peoples from time immemorial, the conflicts that ensued took on symbolic meaning for them. They were cleaning things up. They were getting their house in order. They were settling things. Part of this process involved narrating their exploits as both necessary and moral: they were doing good. But what is very important to recognize in this whole process is that the establishment of whiteness as the moral force of the West was as much a retrospective action as it was a contemporary happening. The West comprised all sorts of people with conflicting and overlapping understandings. The image of the white-hatted cowboy as a sheriff establishing order amid wildness is an invention of movies, television, and dime-store novels. Cowboys were primarily cattlemen, and they included all sorts of people, including Indigenous people, Black people, women, Queer folk, and Asian Americans/Canadians.[44]

The white-washing of cultural diversities is a practice that goes back to colonization and the simplest metaphorizing of black equals bad, white equals good. Part of the lawless spirit of the West was subverted in its prototype version in Africa and its post-type in Western Canada by European adventurers like Edward and Burgon Bickersteth. Although both were connected to projects of land acquisition, their primary vision was of spiritual conversion. For example, Edward Bickersteth had nothing against Africans and, unlike many other Europeans, he did not see the darkness of their skin as a metaphor for the inherent moral condition of their soul.

---

44 See for example: Dulce L. Kersting, *Diversity on the Open Range: Exploring the Experiences of Minority Cowboys During the Nineteenth Century*, Jerry O'Neal Research Fellowship Report (Missoula, MT: Rocky Mountain Cooperative Ecosystem Studies Unit, 2011), 3, 13, 20. https://files.cfc.umt.edu/cesu/NPS/UMT/2011/O'Neal_fellowship_Kersting_report.pdf; Furui Guan, "Chinese Cowboys: A Story of Resilience in the American Old West," preprints, *ScienceOpen Preprints*, 2024, https://doi.org/10.14293/PR2199.000897.v1; Olivia Black, "Representations of Queer Cowboys in History, Literature, and Film" (bachelor's thesis, Providence College, 2025), particularly 8–10, https://digitalcommons.providence.edu/history_undergrad_theses/87/.

For Edward, Christianity was, by default, the truest path to God, but that was a function of practice – of choice – not inherence. His goal was to convince everyone he could to *choose* correctly. I don't know. Maybe there is something in that formula that he offered that was particularly appealing to people who had gone through the Door of No Return. Certainly the centrality of Christianity across multiple communities of African descent in the Americas strongly suggests as much. But equally, there was something in it that also drew the people who were sucked in by the gravitational pull of that door, felt the horror of its gravity, felt its irresistible force lasso them and spin them toward its centre, toward its greedy mouth – only to have some unexpected element deflect them off course and spin them right out of the monster's gaping maw, landing them back on African soil. These people were not lost for generations, did not lose connection to their cultural traditions, or their language, or their ethnic identity. They were stolen into slavery and then by a miracle they could not have predicted, they were returned to the continent of their birth, sometimes only a few days later. But even this narrow escape, this skirting past the ominous forever-door was only the beginning of a profound transformation.

True returns are simply not possible. While they may have begun their journey in Yorubaland (Nigeria) or Asante (Ghana) or Mende (inland Sierra Leone), they were "returned" to Freetown. And Freetown was an engine for Western reconfigurations. In Freetown, they were schooled in English. They were taught to read and cherish the Bible. They were told that people in England, powerful people, who had played a role in their rescue, wanted them to succeed, to know the light of Christ. Although a few of them did manage to reunite with their original communities, most of them had no means of returning to their original homeland (Africa is very large).[45] In a similar way to how Africans in America coalesced around a common cultural identity through their shared historical realities, the Africans who were landed in Freetown amalgamated into a community of multiple ethnicities whose cohering force had two elements: their shared displacement and their ongoing, changed relationship to Africa itself.

One of the most powerful and enduring symbols of this relationship can be seen in the naming processes they underwent. A key task that Edward Bickersteth oversaw was the schooling of the children of so-called recaptives. This, of course, was a religious education and, in that eurocentric way I've mentioned, was meant to showcase Africans' capacity for civilization to those who thought we were inherently barbaric. It's also worth mentioning that organizations like the Church Missionary Society that Bickersteth was affiliated with had a lasting impact. They established schools like Annie Walsh Memorial, Sierra Leone Grammar School, and, at the postsecondary level, Fourah Bay College, which was an educational

---

45 See, for example, Samuel Crowther, who was stolen from Yorubaland in Nigeria but returned to Freetown after the slave ship he was on was intercepted by the British Navy. As an Anglican priest, he established missions in West Africa and eventually returned to Osogun, his original village. He is notable for being the first African to rise to the level of Bishop. See Andrew F. Walls, "Crowther, Samuel Ajayi (A): Foremost African Christian of the Nineteenth Century," *Dictionary of African Christian Biography*, accessed 10 August 2025, https://dacb.org/stories/nigeria/legacy-crowther/.

beacon that served all of West Africa for many years and today is incorporated into the University of Sierra Leone. Although they were established in the nineteenth century, these are schools that my parents attended. As a child, I heard much about the great Annie Walsh Memorial School that my mum attended in her youth. Once, I asked her who this Annie Walsh person was. She shrugged: "Some rich white lady." It was clear that the power of the name was lodged in its own originating memory. The rich white people came to show us another door, different from the one of no return, and their transformational potency has remained in our cultural and historical imagination ever since.

In his diaries, Edward talks about the joy he witnessed in children's faces at learning about the Bible and that they, too, could enjoy all of the heavenly rewards it promised. He impressed upon them the joy their benefactors would receive in learning about their love of Christ. And then he mentions something very curious. He names some of the English benefactors who have donated their money to the cause of educating Africans who had been caught up in slavery, and as part of the process, or maybe part of their education, he bestows these names on the children: Pratt, Biddulph, Martyn. Some of these names I know today. Some of them attended parties at my parents' home. Swirled in dance. Called me nephew.

But, in mentioning these names, Edward Bickersteth also does something very curious. He glosses over the most obvious name of the bunch: his own. Clearly, there were Africans who obtained the name. I have evidence. But for some reason, he says nothing at all about this particular naming. Maybe he was simply being modest. Or maybe it just wasn't important enough to him, as unlikely as that seems (after all, he was literally telling the kids of the importance of their names). Or maybe there just weren't any African Bickersteths yet. Maybe Bickersteth is a name that someone *chose* in the wake of Edward's influential time in Freetown. Or maybe Edward is tiptoeing around some sort of impropriety. Maybe there were no African Bickersteths in 1816 because they were still growing in the womb. Maybe, since he only stayed a few months, he never even knew about the Bickersteth(s) he left behind.

If I sound cynical, I don't mean to. I am sincerely interested to know what happened and I am prepared for all of the answers, tickling to tragic. Actually, it seems to me that Edward was simply too nice a person to pull off an impropriety. It's always a possibility, given his empowered role, as well as the track record of men who find themselves in far-off lands whose inhabitants don't quite count in the way that women like their wives back home do. Have you, for example, heard of the Métis? But though I am covering my bases, I have to confess that it doesn't seem likely that Edward would have engaged in this kind of behaviour. He seems too nice. I might even anecdotally suggest that *niceness* is a standout Bickersteth trait. Years ago, on a flight to the U.K., I had one of those casual airplane friendships with the man seated next to me. We had very little in common but shared a natural curiosity about lifestyles different from our own. As the plane was deploying its landing gear, and we were gamely exchanging contact cards, my new friend did a double-take. "Bickersteth?" he said incredulously, staring at my card. "Your name is Bickersteth?" I felt an old familiar pit in my stomach.

Things had been going so well. Was that old headache still lingering around? Appearing when I least expected? Least wanted it? The Freddy of my Elm Street? "I work for Bickersteths," he continued matter-of-factly. "They own half the town I live in in Kent." The more he spoke, the more I realized he was not questioning the legitimacy of my name. He was genuinely surprised to find himself seated next to someone who had the name of influence and capacity in his community, a name that literally represented his boss, but with whom he had been bantering on equal footing, sharing a laugh, enjoying himself. There was also the fact that our airplane romance had been predicated on our stark differences from each other. He was English; I was Canadian. He had an established career; I was a grad student. The list went on. I'm sure it startled him to see me attached to something so familiar in his world. He finally seemed to process the surprise and gave me a warm smile. His boss, he told me, is actually a very nice man. It was a nice gesture. It was as though he was affirming our own friendly relationship, drawing a figurative consonance between all Bickersteths. We're nice.

I also somewhat made up for my failure to respond to Ursula Bickersteth (yes, she was also nice) who had sent me a letter during my time at UBC Press. I eventually made contact with an actual Bickersteth in England. At the time, I, too, was living in England. I was a graduate student at the University of London. My wife was working as the manager of a high-end shirt shop and so I was primarily caring for our infant son, who had been born in the U.K. Between my studies and my son, I was so busy I hardly had time to pay attention to what was going on around me.

I had recently received an email that made no sense at all to me, outlining my responsibilities for an upcoming meeting that I had no knowledge of. Because I was so busy, I lost track of that email until the day I received a follow-up describing their satisfaction with my performance at this meeting I knew nothing about and had never attended. Now I paused to focus on the details long enough to read the one part of the message that I had skimmed over, indeed, that we all probably skim over: the salutation. It read, "Dear John." I realized that the email was never intended for me. It was not even that someone had sent the email to the wrong address; rather, the correct address had landed in *my* box. I'm not sure I can explain this other than to say it was the early 2000s and (I guess) email technology wasn't as robust as it is today. I'm no programmer so I can't really explain it. All I can say is that I was randomly receiving someone else's emails when I shouldn't have been. One thing about it is that it wasn't one hundred percent random: we shared a last name. At the time, I was on yahoo and my email address was something like bickersteth@yahoo.com. In those days, simply using your last name was enough to get you the email address of your choice. I can't clearly remember John's email address but it was very close to mine, maybe jbickersteth@yahoo.com or something like that. I remember thinking something along the lines of, "well, that shouldn't be possible," but now that I had solved the mystery, I allowed myself to get swept back up in the mayhem of my busy life. A few rogue emails later, I finally got around to emailing John to let him know about this anomaly and forward him his missing emails. It turns out that he had not been missing any messages; duplicates had been sent to my box. What's more, he hardly seemed to care about what we would today see as a serious infringement of privacy and was instead thrilled to have made contact with another Bickersteth.

John was extremely nice in more than one way. It turns out he was retired and something of the family genealogist. Perhaps in an effort to redeem myself with Ursula, I immediately told him that my family was from Sierra Leone. He was completely undaunted. Like Burgon and Edward before him, he had an adventurous spirit and he fondly recognized *all* Bickersteths as legitimately Bickersteth. He enthusiastically told me about various branches he was in contact with in Nigeria. That was something I had no knowledge of. *Nigerian* Bickersteths? He shared with me the family's connections to Church Missions and the many countries that had been therefore

FIG 18 Coat of Arms (52.125) granted to Robert Bickersteth in 1856.

impacted. He gave off no imperialist vibes. He just seemed to have a genuine pleasure in connecting the Bickersteth dots around the world. When he learned I was studying literature, he encouraged me and pointed out that many Bickersteths were writers and many of them were also travellers. "Like you," he prompted. He suggested that if I wrote about my experiences being abroad, I would be joining that tradition. For all of the postcolonial angst it caused me, John made me feel more legitimate in my Bickersteth name than I had ever felt before. When he learned I was wrapping up my studies and we were moving back to North America, he sent me a massive packet full of documents on the history of the Bickersteth name and a family tree that went back to the Middle Ages. He had sent it spontaneously and so the note he scrawled out in his looping spidery cursive expressed his hope that I would receive the package before I had left the country. He wished me all the best. "Warmest wishes to you, Bertrand. On your next visit to the U.K. you must come and stay." He was so nice.

So maybe Edward Henry Bickersteth was just nice. His orientation was eurocentric, but his intention was egalitarian (through Christ). The best scenario, then, for my first Bickersteth, is that someone, let's call him Abiola, found himself a pawn in the wars between Yoruba factions. Swept up in a military raid, he was sold to Europeans in exchange for weapons to serve their war. This was the worst thing to ever happen to Abiola. He was a fun-loving character, boisterous and demanding with his family, but loyal and full of exuberance. He enjoyed *fufu* lathered in palm oil and he loved the striking tang of palm wine tapped from the tree. He lived for song and dance and was known by everyone as an enthusiastic celebrant at any occasion. He prided himself on inventing new dance steps for festive times. One of them caught on in popularity and he smiled to see even the young people mimic his long, sweeping step followed by two joyful half-circles of the foot. Sometimes, his enthusiasm tipped the scales into frenetic, overexcited territory. But he never crossed that line far enough that anyone doubted he would eventually come to his senses. He always eventually did. Abiola was chained to his fellow captives and made to walk miles until they reached the coast. The sight of the sea terrified him. He had never seen it before and as far as he knew he had reached the end of the earth. Nothing of this mortal world could lie beyond that flat and shimmering expanse. In a sense, he was right: nothing human lay in store for him once he crossed that haunted plane. In another sense, what lay before him was only far too human in its appetite, its solipsism, its fear of the other. A man whose skin was transparent like a ghost's approached him with a stick of some sort, and as he was held down by other Ghostmen, the first pressed the end of the stick onto his chest. The pain was excruciating. He screamed. He passed out. He was brought on board the *Betsey*, a ship that had already held hundreds of Africans, and the smell of their confinement, their struggles, assaulted Abiola the instant he was shoved below deck into the ominous hold.[46]

46 The *Betsey* was one of a number of slave ships that was constructed in Canada, in this case, Newfoundland. Like so many stories in this text, there is no scope for us to properly pursue this particular trail, but I urge you to look into it yourself.

For two weeks he was in hell, tossed along the seas, stifled in the heat and stench of human fluid, excrement, blood. It was there, in the hold, that he realized he had certainly crossed into a world he did not belong. He felt the fury of the gods in every toss of the sea, every baffling encounter with the Ghostmen who had no interest in his suffering. A stubborn man, never one to accept the limits before him, he began to hatch a plan to fight back against the Ghostmen with the men chained nearest him. Then, as they were about to execute the insurrection, they heard a commotion on deck. There was cannon fire and excited voices. The women, who were generally not chained in the hold and had access to the deck, appeared to have already instigated something! They took advantage of the distraction to work at their manacles and, with the help of some of the women, freed themselves. When they reached the deck, they emerged into a battle raging in full. Ghostmen from another ship were boarding and attacking their captors. After a bloody battle, the new Ghostmen and the freedom-claiming Africans took control of the ship and returned it to the African coast.

Abiola found himself in Freetown, the most cosmopolitan place he had ever landed: he was surrounded by a plurality of people, languages, and customs. He was grateful to be back on land that he never thought he would see again. The Ghostmen who had fought with him on the ship commended his bravery and told him he was specially recognized by their God. Abiola wanted to know more about this God who had shown favour on him, allowing him to cross back through the Door of No Return. A Ghostman named *Bickersteth* showed him a book that spoke words of power and told him that he was *blessed* by the power of this book. In the coming weeks, Abiola settled in Freetown, found a loving partner whom he married, and tried to learn the Ghostmen's language. But it was difficult. He never quite got the hang of it. Occasionally, he would finger the marks that had been burned into his chest, just over his heart. Bickersteth had told him it was a "letter" from his language. Abiola did not understand what this "letter" was exactly, but he felt a deep compulsion to erase it from his skin. He often traced it with a sad finger, as though he could do just that.[47]

Once, while he rubbed at the mark, he was surprised to feel an odd familiarity in its pattern. He rubbed at it again and again, trying to capture the meaning of the feeling when all of a sudden he recognized it. Its straight line and two swirls were an echo of the sweeping dance step he had invented just before the calamity of war had struck.

47 Archive image courtesy Katrina H.B. Keefer. "Liberated African Department; Register Nos 7508–9758 [1815–1816]," Sierra Leone Public Archives, British Library Endangered Archives Programme, EAP443/1/17/5, https://eap.bl.uk/archive-file/EAP443-1-17-5.

FIG 19 Abiola Traces His Past. Katrina H.B. Keefer/Author.

He was in awe. How did the Ghostmen know this? Was it their God? He had for so long hated this mark that his flesh could never forget.

Now, it remembered something entirely different. Maybe, because of this, he also never forgot *Bickersteth* and the *blessings* he had talked about. When Abiola's first son was born, he cried with all the passion he used to expel at joyful celebrations. For the first time since he had been captured in the Yoruba wars, he got to his feet and he danced. Now his feet remembered what his flesh could not forget: the graceful straight-backed step, the two glorious swirls of joy. He called his son Ekundayo William Bickersteth, in honour of the Ghostman who shared his *blessings* with him. He wished all of his descendants the same transformational tears he had shed for generations to come.

This is the best version of the story, one in which the name Bickersteth is a special category of *choosing*, reflecting agency and transformation together. I don't know if it is the right story. Documents on Africans who were returned to Sierra Leone from slave ships are incomplete and difficult to search through. The *SlaveVoyages* database provides a lot of information on the ships used in the slave trade and even provides limited information on the Africans who were landed in Freetown, including their African names and any marks noted on their skin.[48] Similarly, the Register of Liberated Africans, housed in the British Library's

---

48 "Voyages: Trans-Atlantic," SlaveVoyages, accessed 6 February 2026, https://www.slavevoyages.org/voyage/trans-atlantic#voyages

Endangered Archives Program, contains brief information on the people who were returned from slave ships to Freetown. But there is no way to connect this information to anyone who consequently chose (or inherited) a European name. There is no way to know when and how that specific transformation took place. These are the gaps we must sacrifice to the imagination, to the arts, to poetry. These are the *choosings* of agency that we must acknowledge took place. Maybe Freeman is a name that a Black rancher's family in East-central Alberta had imposed on them. Maybe it is a name they chose. And maybe, in so choosing, they *returned* to it. Maybe, in the same manner, Bickersteth is simply a name one of my unnameable ancestors returned to. Though I suffered much confusion and embarrassment about my name when I was younger, I now clearly recognize the possibilities that others failed to see – like the tension inherent in African family trees that are marked by European names – as an impossible return that is a particular historical legacy. I need not feel shamed by Ursula Bickersteth's unsuspecting presumptions or my colleagues at UBC Press who could never have known the turmoil they caused in me when they wondered at the possibility of a family link. Strangely, I think it was a reality that John Bickersteth sensed in his enthusiasm for all Bickersteths and is reflected in the poetry of the name Ekundayo, a Yoruba name I bequeathed to my son, which means *my tears have become joy*. In other words, impossible returns *are* the possibilities.

MY TEARS HAVE BECOME JOY

The final Black cowboy's cattle brand I would like to share with you is one belonging to Charles Dyson. Dyson was a farmer, a rancher, and the community blacksmith in Pincher Creek, Alberta. His family story seems split between two remarkable possibilities. The first is that they lived as free Black people during the era of slavery. Dyson's mother, Rachel, was born in 1824 or so in upstate New York, which strongly suggests her family was free. Dyson's father, Charles Henry, was from Baltimore originally. Maryland was a slave state but Baltimore was a unique city in that it held the largest population of free Black people in the country.[49] In fact, there were far more free Black people in Baltimore than enslaved ones. This suggests that Charles Henry, like his wife, was likely free, despite the prevailing presence of slavery. If true, it is a remarkable family legacy for Dyson to claim. The other possibility is equally remarkable: the Dysons are emblematic of freedom-seeking Black families who found their way to agency through the historic Underground Railroad.

Here I want to be cautious about what I'm celebrating exactly. The one element of Black history that is regularly admitted in Canada is the nation's role in the Underground Railroad. But Canada is too quick to frame this history as a reflection of its

49 For more on the paradoxical nature of Baltimore's status, see, for example, T. Stephen Whitman, *The Price of Freedom: Slavery and Manumission in Baltimore and Early National Maryland* (New Haven, CT: Yale University Press, 1997), 94.

own tolerance and benevolence in opposition to the racism of the United States, which legalized the practice of slavery. History as a gesture of solipsism doesn't interest me, particularly in this context. I shouldn't have to remind you, for example, that Canada also had legalized slavery, nor that many Black people *returned* to the U.S. immediately after the abolition of slavery there, a phenomenon that suggests things were not so attractive in "tolerant and benevolent" Canada that it encouraged them to stay here. For me, the significance of the Underground Railroad here is in its demonstration of the persistent claims on human dimensionality that Black people made. What they were seeking was not a simple relation between slavery and freedom, where freedom was the inverted prize to slavery. They were seeking the varieties of ways in which people express their humanity from under the cosh of limitations that restricted who they were and how they chose to live out extra/ordinary possibilities, such as family, relationship, and love.

Black people who were enslaved regularly and repeatedly sought ways out of slavery. They concocted ideas together, they colluded with allies, they asserted their visions. Although Baltimore was largely populated with free Black people, slavery was still the legal reality and, as a port city, slaves were still regularly sold into servitude in the South. Free Black people were often accused of being runaway slaves and threatened with being returned into slavery. The topic was particularly heated in the years leading up to 1850, which saw the Fugitive Slave law enacted. This was a law that shifted the onus of proof onto the accused. In other words, if a

Black person was accused of being a runaway slave, the accuser no longer had to provide proof; instead, it was up to the Black person to show evidence that they had *not* escaped from slavery, which had a very high bar that was almost never met. This resulted in many innocent people being falsely forced into slavery and created an atmosphere of tension and antagonism among the free Black residents of Baltimore. During the 1840s, Dyson's father made his way to Syracuse, New York, which was a prominent terminus on the Underground Railroad. This decision strongly suggests his desire to transcend an environment in which slavery prevails. Further to that, after marrying Rachel and starting a family, they all moved to Chatham, Ontario, which was yet another terminus on the Underground Railroad and had a large population of Black people who had come from the U.S. This pattern of movement, from Baltimore to Syracuse to Chatham, is deeply entrenched in the histories of migration that were made possible through the Underground Railroad.

However, the most consistent narration of the Underground Railroad in Canada overlooks its most important element. The dynamic is not a binary between slavery and freedom. This particular binary blinds Canadians to the obvious. Slavery didn't just prevent "freedom" as a concept that limited Black people's actions. Slavery dehumanized us. The heart of being human is social connection, meaningful community. From the start, slavery terrorized the meaningful connections between enslaved Africans. They were forced apart, prevented from sharing space with members of their own ethnic groups, depriving them of their customs, their languages, their world views. In the Americas they were further forced out of relation with each other. Family members could be sold at a moment's notice; women could be raped; parentage was erased. Even attempts to commune spiritually were either refused or sporadically offered, and always heavily regulated. The response to these kinds of impositions was to vigorously seek to rebuild community, family, and relationship.

John Ware's story may be inspiring to many Canadians because he "overcame slavery" but this is an abstract honour. The obvious is missed. Rarely is the centrality of his family relationships considered: that he had five children, that he had a loving wife, that she came from a large and loving family, itself connected to various ongoing Black communities in Alberta as well as in Ontario, where they came from. Rarely do people think of this very specific, very necessary achievement in Ware's life: the re-fusing of networks of love through an ongoing and living complex of friendships, family, faith, and community. Witness, one of the most common acts that formerly enslaved Black people pursued after abolition was to marry. What does that tell you about the dimensionality of Black people? What does that tell you about the binary dynamic of slavery and freedom? Yes, the Underground Railroad is a centrally important vehicle of Black agency and Canada should be proud of its participation. But, frankly, it is lazy thinking to simply reduce the value of the Underground Railroad to the conduit of "freedom." Dyson's family may have been enslaved at some point and moved to align with the possibilities of agency, or, they may have been free Black people who chose to *preserve their family* by removing themselves from the unjustified threat of slavery. Either way, the family's story is a remarkable one.

Charles Dyson was born into this context in 1844 or 1845, in Syracuse, New York. In 1850, the family was still located in Syracuse; in 1861, they were settled in Chatham, Ontario. But by 1870, they were back in the U.S. It appears that the Dyson family is included among the statistics of Black people who did not see the need to stay in Canada once slavery in the U.S. was abolished. Curiously, though, while the family resettles in Barry County, Michigan, Charles, who was about twenty-seven years old at this point, chose to stay in Canada. It may have been that he had spent the significant years of his childhood there and now felt "Canadian" enough to want to stay when the rest of the family returned to the U.S.[50] Who knows? Like so much of Black history, we are forced into speculation because the gaps outnumber the facts. But I think I have one clear indication of what might have kept him rooted in the Great White North. In 1870, he married a local girl, Liza Jefferson, and he never left Canada after that.

By 1900, the couple reappeared in Pincher Creek, Alberta. Pincher Creek is cattle country and so it is no surprise that Charles eventually took up ranching. His cattle brand first appears in the 1900 *North West Brand Book*.

50 Remember, the Fugitive Slave Act came into effect in 1850. At this point, no free Black person was safe from the threat of slavery. This legal event may have been the trigger for the Dyson family's move to Ontario, which suggests Charles may have been living in Canada from the time he was roughly six years old.

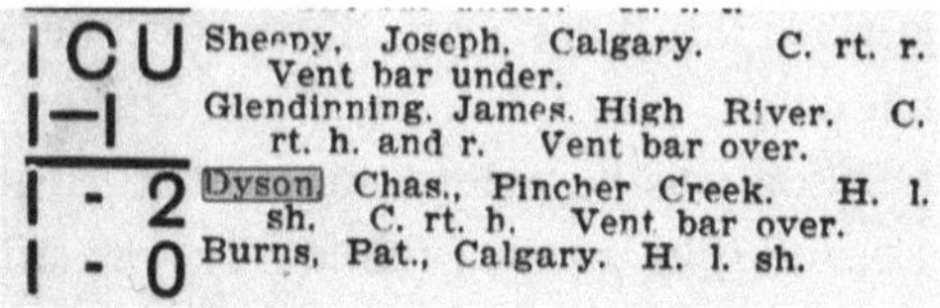

Sheepy, Joseph, Calgary. C. rt. r. Vent bar under.
Glendinning, James, High River. C. rt. h. and r. Vent bar over.
Dyson, Chas., Pincher Creek. H. l. sh. C. rt. h. Vent bar over.
Burns, Pat., Calgary. H. l. sh.

As a contributor of Black cattle brands in Alberta, Charles Dyson stands out for two very important reasons. First, as a blacksmith and as someone who had a cattle brand, it is very likely that he forged his own branding iron. This is remarkable to me because it reveals the conception of brand designs for what it is: artistry. I see Dyson as a fellow poet, a scribe whose language was molten metal, whose medium was fire.

For me, this makes Dyson seem like Hephaestus, the Greek God who forged great weapons and armour for the heroes, notably Achilles and Aeneas (in his Roman incarnation, Vulcan). He was, too, a lame God who had been cast from the heights of Mount Olympus by Zeus, his own father, for the simple reason, it would seem, that he was ugly. In some stories, Hephaestus is the sole creation of Hera, Zeus's wife, and *that's* why he is hurled from heaven's heights. Zeus is angered by her creative independence and immediately takes a dislike to the son who is not his son. To cement the relationship, it is emphasized that Hephaestus is ugly and even Hera is embarrassed by her own creation (in some versions, *she* is the one who tosses him away for this reason). Either way, he is forcibly ejected from heaven. In most accounts, his ignominious landing injures his foot permanently, which sometimes makes him something of a laughingstock to the other gods. In this way, I strongly identify with him.

FIG 20 Charles Dyson, "Bar One-Two". Note, beneath is a brand owned by Pat Burns, one of the Calgary Stampede's Big Four founders.

I often felt as though Alberta, my parent who is not my parent, rejected me growing up. Equally, it is a powerful metaphor for the Black experience in general. Marked by this thing called Blackness, we are also marred by it. At the same time, like Hephaestus, we find ways of transcending it, of transforming it, of creating.

In this way, maybe it is also fitting to think of Dyson as a version of Ogun, the West African Yoruba God. Like Hephaestus, Ogun is something of a blacksmith; he has access to and forges with iron; he is a technological god, who provides the way forward when no clear path seems available. The difference between the two is that Ogun is not a victim of circumstances in the way that Hephaestus is. True to many Greek myths, Hephaestus is a character in a drama full of characters. The challenges that he faces have to do with the personalities and ambitions of other – more powerful gods – around him. His solution is metaphorical: he creates weapons out of his dire circumstances. But the problem he emblematizes is purely human: you're ugly and we don't like you. In the case of the Yoruba God, the problem is circumstantial: it is simply the nature of reality that occasionally there are obstacles to face. Sometimes, this is depicted as a literal bush space between Heaven and Earth that the gods are struggling to find their way through. Ogun seizes iron from the earth, almost in an act of determined theft, and by creating tools like machetes, forges a path through the impenetrable bush for the gods to make their way. In the West African tradition, it is the problem that is metaphorical: life has obstacles we cannot avoid. This has nothing to do with personalities or the drama of characters; it is simply the existential realities of the world we must face.

I think of Charles Dyson as Black Hephaestus because in my mind he is a hybrid of the Greek and Yoruba traditions. In an oddly fitting way, the new hybridized label obscures its African origins. Ogun + Hephaestus = Black Hephaestus. This is the inevitable result of our North American context. The fact of Blackness – the historical reconfiguring of our identities – is the unavoidable existential reality on this continent. It is scrawled over top of any preceding dimensions. And it happens to any African – and most dark-skinned people – who comes to this country from elsewhere, regardless of their own preexisting histories, ethnicities, traditions, or languages. They become palimpsestically Black. This is one way of looking at the Wild West of human relations that this continent perpetrates. Once relocated here, Black people are caught up in a forced relation with white people making meaning for themselves. This makes us subject to all manner of illogical categorizations, from the petty – being placed at the bottom of hierarchies of beauty – to the profound – having the legitimacy of our humanity questioned – even as pettiness and profundity are collapsed as one. Charles Dyson's historic presence clears the way for me, provides me with a path through an impenetrable set of circumstances that also involves stealing the language of burned flesh.

FIG 21 My Path Through "Bar 1–2."

I said that Dyson stands out in two ways. The first is that he is the forger of his own branding iron, Black Hephaestus. The second is that he is always with his wife, Liza, the woman who kept him rooted in Canada when the rest of his family went back to the U.S. Charles and Liza were married in Ontario and made the move west to Alberta at the end of the nineteenth century. Eventually, they started a ranch in Pincher Creek and Charles registered his brand. If you will indulge me, I would like to suggest that Liza is the key to unlocking Charles's brand. Reading this cattle brand presents a challenging opacity. All of the cattle brands I've been exploring have their particular difficulties, and Dyson's brand is particularly challenging because it is composed of numbers. These numbers don't appear to bear any direct relation to anything obvious either, like the year of his birth or some other straightforward talisman. Much like today's 6-7 (which you will have no understanding of if you are reading this in 2026 and you are over the age of forty), a basic sequence is suggested; in fact, it is the most basic sequence, the initiating numbers at the start of the entirety of numbers. But, with no supporting context at all, the simplicity itself is rendered as an inscrutable complexity. Because of who I am, I would like to offer some poetic guidance toward understanding this brand. To my eye, there is a third, fundamental mark to the brand. This is the bar between the two numbers. In the language of cattle brands, bars are very common and they decorate all sorts of well-known historic brands, such as the Bar U Ranch in Southern Alberta, and the Bar S Ranch near Nanton, AB, or the brand mark, "Bar 7 Square S" (often mistaken for 75), which has been in the family of a friend of mine since the early 1900s.

Part of the difficulty with deciphering brands is that they very often convey some sort of insider knowledge; you have to be part of the community or, as with my friend's family brand, part of the family, to fully know the brand. And the bar is a fundamental starting point with cattle brands. Every straight line begins with a bar. But also, it is the cattle thief's main tool. The running iron is a simple bar that can be applied to existing brands, changing their original design. For example, a bar added to the bottom of a capital F changes the letter into an E. Cattle thieves would judiciously add their simple strokes to existing brands and thus falsely alter the ownership and deviously claiming the cattle for themselves. Like it or not, folks, this, too, is poetics. You've been seeing it in action. Frederick Hall's *F* plus Charles Dyson's Bar progresses my alphabet, illustrating my point.

FIG 22 A Trace of Dyson's Bars. **FIG 23** The Running Iron's Way with Words.

I can cut the inscrutability of Green Walters's yoke in half, flip it, and make it the Jumping-off point for my brand of poetics by simply adding a line.

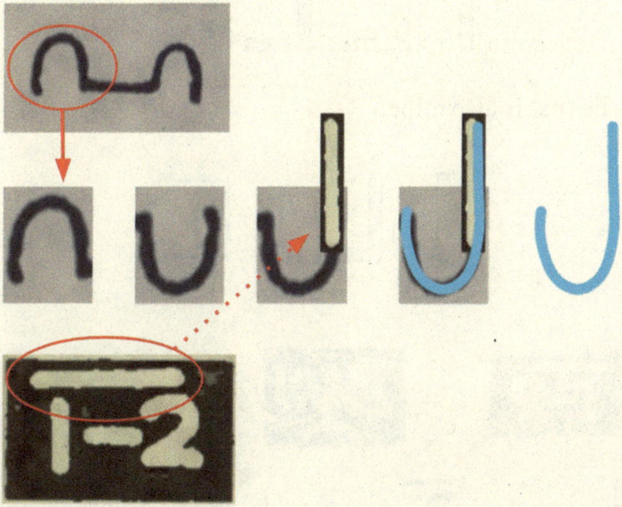

I can assert myself as a subject self when I realign Dyson's bar as mine.

FIG 24 The Jumping-Off Point of Brand Poetics.

FIG 25 "M|ne."

When I add a line to his line and have it lie down, I create the beginning of a new line.

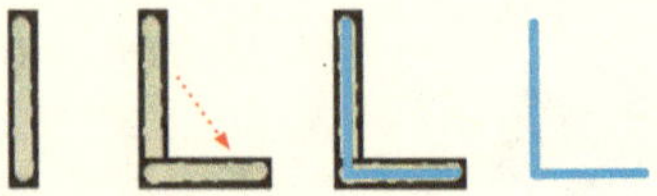

A new lie that is also mine.

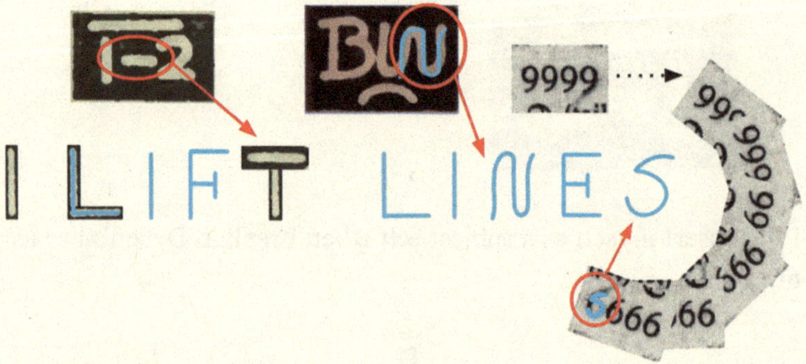

FIG 26 "I Lies Down."
FIG 27 "A Trace of the Truth."
FIG 28 The Poetics of Black Cattle Brands.

These are the poetics of Black brands that I choose to lift to the level of theft. The simple bar is the fundamental line that begins everything by palimpsestically erasing what was there before. In the language of Black cattle brands, the bar is the only mark that can add and subtract at the same time. This is not an idle or passing observation. Note, in cattle brands the bar is a joining symbol that can literally link. You can see it in the case of the Bar U brand, in which the bar and the U become a unit, though not actually connected. It is certainly the case with a brand like S-S, in which the bar literally links the two letters together, like two criminals, or captives, slave to slave.

This is the clear adding power of the bar. But bars can also subtract, particularly when they are enacted by running irons. With a running iron, I can take the *c* branded on your cattle and turn it into a *d* and then, with two more strokes, it can become *d7*. Now you've lost your cattle to me. Your brand is erased. My additions equal your subtraction.

FIG 29 Two versions of "S Bar S."

This, too, if you will allow me, is the poetry of Dyson's cattle brand. The evidence is in his move to Alberta. Once here, he did a number of impressive things: he became Pincher Creek's first blacksmith, he started a ranch with his wife, he designed and registered his own cattle brand, and he witnessed his wife register a brand under her name as well. Even John Ware — who acquired multiple brands and dispersed them throughout his family — did not hold a brand side by side with his wife, who held her own. This circumstance surely makes Charles and Liza Dyson the *most* cattle couple of all the Black cattle ranchers in the West. I'm still looking, but at this point I can probably say that Liza Dyson was one of the few Black women in Western Canada who owned her own cattle brand — the first being Nettie Ware, when she was barely ten years old. When I first spotted Liza's brand in the brand book, it seemed to strongly evoke something of the Dyson name to me.

Dyson Mrs. E. J., Pincher Creek; l. r.

The brand is composed of an inverted — or upside down — P, followed by a number 7, all over an inverted rafter symbol. Inverted letters, more colourfully, can also be called "crazy" letters. Rafters are normally placed above other figures, like the roof of an A-frame house, but brands often play around with positioning. In this case, the rafter is being a little "crazy" too, being upside down as well as acting somewhat like the "floor" of the brand. The fact that

FIG 30 "Crazy P 7 Inverted Rafter," Eliza Dyson's brand.

the letter P was crazy, strongly suggesting a *d*, along with the coincidence of the 7's somewhat analogous shape to the letter *y* (particularly the similarly angled backbone of them both), immediately struck me as an attempt to approach the first two letters of the Dyson family name.

But this interpretation was soon countered by another reality. In the 1907 published brand book, I came across the same brand registered to John Hardy. Normally, this is not a large problem. Identical brands were often registered by different people so long as they placed it in a different location on the animal's body. This is why you will see "right thigh" or "left flank" mentioned as part of the brand information. Also, though, if the two brand owners live reasonably far away from each other — such that their cattle could never interact and be confused with one another — it was considered acceptable for their brands to be completely identical. I have seen many identical brands in various brand books, but they were often located in different provinces or in opposite regions of the same province. In the late nineteenth and early twentieth centuries, these distances would have been impossible to overcome without weeks' worth of travel. In the case of Liza Dyson's brand, though, the two owners were both located in Pincher Creek, Alberta. This could only mean one thing: Liza had purchased cattle from John Hardy and had the existing brand registered in her name as part of the transfer. I was only slightly disappointed that the brand wasn't her original design. It's still a great accomplishment, a great story: this Black woman in Southern Alberta was part of the cattle industry and there is a record of her participation.

Moreover, she participated as part of a Black family, a power couple of Black ranching deities, Hephaestus and Aphrodite, growing their stock, expanding their brand. Let me quickly point out, however, that Aphrodite does not make a neat comparison here because in the Greek myths her marriage to Hephaestus was arranged and marked by infidelity. I do prefer to think of her in her Roman incarnation of Venus because Black Venus was a Civil Rights symbol that artists such as Margaret Burroughs and Romare Bearden invoked powerfully.[51] But, like the secret language of Black cattle brands, "Venus" courts more than one Black history, bringing to mind for instance Sarah Baartman, who was paraded around Europe as the Hottentot Venus, and is not easily or uncomplicatedly accessed in any context.

Mainly, though, the analogy doesn't work for me because the Dysons seemed like such a solid couple. I said that Charles Dyson did a number of impressive things when he moved to Alberta, and the most impressive thing, by far, is that he fell for his Black Venus, Liza. Twice. There is an odd blip in the historical documents. After Charles and Liza move from Ontario to Alberta, there is a mention of the husband and wife getting married *again*. When I first saw this, I had to shake my head.

---

51 Burroughs and Bearden are two Black artists whose work ranges over several decades but was especially impactful during the social upheavals of the 1960s. For Margaret Burroughs's work, see https://www.nga.gov/artworks/143183-black-venus. For an example of Romare Bearden's work, see https://www.kemperartmuseum.wustl.edu/collection/search-results/wu-1994-01-romare-bearden-american-19111988-black-venus-1968.

FIG 31 *Black Venus* (1957) by Margaret Burroughs (courtesy National Gallery of Art).

Wow, I thought to myself. What a loverman Dyson was. Not content to get hitched to his Canadian gal in Ontario, he doubled down on his love and renewed the whole process in Alberta. I loved this idea of fealty to love, this longevity, this ever-enduring commitment. Fittingly, Dyson's brand is also notable for being one of the longest-standing Black brands. He registered it in 1900 and it shows up in brand books for the next twenty years. None of the other Black brands I've discussed (or identified so far) offer this level of longevity. In this way, they conform to the general ephemerality of Black history, but in this one very specific way my Black Hephaestus bucks this trend. Why wouldn't this long-distance competitor in love persistently prove his presence, his particular dimensionality? *He got married to the same woman twice*!

Except that he didn't. On 1 November 1870, Charles Dyson was married to Eliza Jefferson in Chatham, Ontario, but on 6 June 1901, when Charles married Eliza again, this time she was called Eliza Johnson. It is the most extraordinary coincidence that is nothing more than ordinary in that particular day and age. Elizabeth is a common name, less so today, but not much less. Eliza is almost never a diminutive version today, but it was ubiquitous in that form in Charles Dyson's day. There really is no mystery behind his two marriages: they were two different Elizas. But what happened to the first Eliza? Eliza Jefferson from Chatham? I imagine her as a childhood sweetheart. There is no clear evidence of how long the Dysons lived in Chatham before heading back to the U.S. – it could have been anywhere from a few years to nearly two decades.

And if it was the latter period, Dyson would very likely consider Chatham his home and Liza Jefferson his hometown girl. But as usual, Black history is a reluctant guest at the party of clear facts. Instead of mingling at the centre of the crowd, it hangs back, speaking only shyly and intermittently, uncertain of the company it is meant to keep. Hence, mysteries abound: in 1871, for example, there is no sign of Charles in the census. Eliza is there, in Chatham, married (her name is now Dyson), but Charles was somehow missed – or missing. It was probably nothing more than Dyson was out and the census enumerator did not account for everyone in the household. But this seems strange. Why wouldn't *Eliza* account for him? Why would he not have somehow turned up on the census anyway? Was there discord between the newlyweds? Had something already happened – barely a year into their marriage – that tainted Eliza's willingness when the enumerator inquired after her husband (she is, after all, indicated as *married* on the census)? Whatever the reason, Charles Dyson is a non-presence in 1871, until he pops back up – with Eliza – in the 1881 census. No apologies. No explanation. That is the way of historical documents. And then, after that – again with no explanation – it is Eliza who takes over as the non-presence. The 1881 census is her last appearance in history. This is why it was so easy for me to assume the couple was still a couple when I located them in Alberta in the 1900s. People pop in and out of censuses all the time. In this way, censuses are both the official records and the magic acts of our collective past. And part of the magic is built into the genealogical and research process. In other words, part of the deception in the magic act includes me: I didn't locate the Dysons in the east and then travel with them forward in time as they travelled west to Pincher Creek. I found Charles Dyson in Alberta *first*; I lovingly located his cattle brand in the 1900 Brand Book; I saw his wife's name in a later brand book; and *then* I traced their trajectory back in time. Eliza (Johnson) Dyson was *my* first Eliza Dyson. It was the most natural thing in the world for me to assume the Eliza I saw in 1881 was the same Eliza I saw in 1906; that she was the same Eliza Dyson living (alone?) in Chatham one year; that she was the same Eliza who married her Chatham man in a Methodist church the year before.

But she wasn't. Eliza Jefferson was Dyson's hometown honey from Chatham. Eliza Johnson was not even from Canada. She had been living in Chicago before marrying Charles. In fact, she had already been married previously. Her maiden name is actually Reed and she was born in Battle Creek, Michigan, a stone's throw away from where Charles's family had moved after they left Chatham. In a weird way, she too might be considered a hometown gal to the Dyson family in general. Who knows, maybe this marriage was arranged after all between families familiar with each other. (Maybe Black Venus *is* her appropriate divine avatar.) The archives say very little about these intimate details. But some things can be determined. We know that Charles had been in Pincher Creek since at least 1891, and we know that this represents a ten-year gap since his first bride last appears in the documents. As for her disappearance, Charles himself whispers the sad truth from the archives. In the 1891 federal census, Dyson admits a *W* next to his name: he was a widower and Eliza was dead. If she had somehow lived to 1891, she would have barely cracked her forties. I suspect she did not get even that far, that she died while the couple was still in Ontario, that her death, maybe, precipitated an irretrievable change in Charles, which led him to do the impossible, even when his parents had beckoned from Michigan decades earlier: leave his beloved Chatham for good.

How did Eliza die? What took her life so young? History peers shyly at us but keeps quiet. Dyson had moved west like all of the era's aspiring opportunists, but he was striving to escape the shadow that had fallen over his heart as much as he was moving toward something new. He was no longer young; he was approaching his fifties; he was changed by the shadow over his heart. And soon, I will show you proof. Nevertheless, it was a new beginning for him, and he made the most of it. He was self-sufficient and pioneering; he became the town's first blacksmith. He built a log cabin for himself that was remembered in the 1940s and seen as historic. He was a member of the community, as demonstrated by his many mentions in the *Pincher Creek Echo*. Maybe he rekindled something of his old sense of home in this new town in Alberta. Maybe this new departure rekindled an old dimension in him and he felt the flames of love, for Eliza, again.

Maybe. I don't know. There is a famous story concerning my namesake, the philosopher and mathematician Bertrand Russell, and his collaborator Alfred North Whitehead. In their influential text *Principia Mathematica*, they set out to prove the symbolic logic of the basic equation 1 + 1 = 2, which they do, but it takes them several hundred pages. In other words, for all its simplicity, *one and one* is not a straightforward equation. The poetry flowing in me understands this wrinkle through the logic of running irons. It tells me that bars are always important. Bars can be barriers, even forms of banishment. When we say "bar none," we invoke it as a counter to itself. We reach for it as a standard; it can be high or low, depending on if you're being aspirational or critical. In the language of brands, the bar links, it joins, but sometimes it also subtracts. And, maybe, as I apply my own running iron – my own bar – to this narrative, I am altering Dyson's narrative with my own mark (of course I am: I have been leaving my marks all over history in this book). But maybe this double way of seeing bars – as additions and subtractions – is an appropriate way of reading his brand. I apply the poetry of my running iron to Dyson's bar and alter it, without altering it, from a bar sign to a minus sign. In so doing, I alter Dyson's brand from a cipher of meaning to a decipherable brand, from random numbers to a balancing equation. Now, I no longer see "one bar two." I see one and two *and* one *minus* two. The bar becomes its doubled self, the linking *and* the subtraction at once. The gathering force of belonging (a pseudo roundup of the everyday) and the obtruding barrier of exclusion at the same time.

Charles Dyson did many impressive things when he moved to Alberta. But, maybe, according to my running iron poetry at least, the most impressive thing he did was to acknowledge his two Lizas, both of whom he loved, both of whom he was joined to – a situation that could only exist simultaneously in his brand.

And this doubling is a dimensionality of love that is elevated by the brand. As much as the 2 can represent his two Lizas, it is even more powerfully representative of a state of union, something that he lost when he lost Liza Jefferson to death. The 1 is not simply Charlie himself, but the bachelor minus the state of union he aspires toward. The bar in this context is the most basic mark because it signals the fullness of his dimensionality. The one is always connected to the two, even when it cannot be connected to both. Even when one Liza gets subtracted from the equation, the bachelor is still the man of matrimony. The basic bar speaks to a plurality that is only too human. In this way, Dyson has advanced Green Walters's Double Doke. Dyson's "doubledness" is the simultaneous plus and minus of belonging. But it is not a state of belonging that is in any way beholden to impositions from white society. It is not a navigation of obstacles to assert or prove the validity of one's humanity against the prevailing standard. In Dyson's case, the proof is in the equation. He was born to a family whose defining impulse was to realize the freedom in love. If seeking companionship, union, intimate communing is the highest bar for human relationship, then it is also the most basic, common impulse of all people and thus the lowest bar. This is the truest dimensionality of our humanity. It defies both the rules of geometry and the laws of physics. It is simultaneously local and universal. It is physically embodied and geographically displaced. And, maybe, when it is flattened into something like Blackness, maybe, it is still perfectly capable of figuring out its own undeniable brand of love.

MY JOY HAS BECOME TEARS

In the 1980s, when the world was not so thoroughly interconnected as social media's present-day has enabled, a returnee from a visit "home" was an event to celebrate by the Prairie Africans of my Alberta. This meant the delivery of many long-missed items that the average Canadian doesn't even know they're missing, but that was soul-restoring and regenerative to my parents' generation. This would mean *actual* palm oil was now accessible. No more canned tomato paste as a weakly-analogous substitute. For a couple of weekends my mom would busily prepare Krio culinary classics like *plassass* and *granat sup* in what she called the *proper* way. "Ah," I thought to myself, "so all along we've been eating another version of a hodgepodge, pinching ingredients that don't actually belong to us." My own personal teenage angst was not so thick a fog, though, that I couldn't see the joy these reconnections brought to the displaced West Africans. And nothing seemed to encapsulate that more than music. They were thrilled by the latest musical craze from Freetown and wore out the grainy cassette tapes from weeks of replay. Funny enough, though, the party music they seemed to favour mostly came from the other side of the ocean. For a lot of my childhood, my parents had been happy to bounce along to dance songs coming out of the Caribbean: the eighties reggae vibes of Black Uhuru; the soul-inflected crooning of Gregory Isaacs, especially his hit "Night Nurse;" and particularly the sizzling rhythms of soca music from Trinidad. Arrow's "Hot, Hot, Hot" drenched our living room dance floors long before Buster Poindexter reintroduced his slightly cabaret, slightly campy version to mainstream audiences. Mighty Sparrow, a calypso master who switched it up with soca in the eighties had a massive hit with a song called "Soca Pressure," whose insistent chorus thrummed in my head years after those eighties house parties. Their ultimate choice, though, had to have been "Tiny Winey," a classic "jump-up" by the Jamaican group Byron Lee & the Dragonaires. This was played at every gathering with energy and enthusiasm and was almost certain to get our parents urging the kids to join them "just this once." We did. But we feigned exasperation to keep our teen street cred.

It was "Tiny Winey" that was playing on the night my family was throwing a party for Aunty Biola. The evening had been a roaring success, even when her husband, my Uncle Biola, tipped the evening toward something menacing, something approaching sinister. And me, in my confused frustration about which identity I could authentically own, had been so seduced by this glimpse into an alternate universe where my uncle was still somehow both in Calgary, on the winter prairies, and in Sierra Leone, acting the part of a "real" African man, that I had completely forgotten about the purpose of the party. And I should not have forgotten that. I should have been aware of how jubilantly my aunt was being celebrated, how everything was tinged with the prickle of relief, how, even, purposefully and intently my aunt, aglow in the atmosphere of rejoice, gazed at me.

My Aunt Biola was unlike her husband in so many ways. She was orderly and timely; he was instinctive and abrupt. She was a thoughtful planner; he was a reactive volcano. She was a meticulous manager of events; he was a hopeless, helpless victim of circumstances. In one way, though, they were very suited to each other. They both tended to be traditional in their responsibilities to each other. Uncle Biola was the breadwinner, handled anything to do with the car, punished the children, and dealt with door-to-door salesmen and telemarketers. Aunt Biola managed the household, did not have a driver's licence, knew every woman on the block, and always had Uncle Biola's supper ready when he got home. In this way, their inversions marked the shape of the puzzle pieces of their shared lives: mysteriously compatible. Part of the mystery was that they both shared strong and stubborn personalities and could be unrelenting in the positions they took up. Occasionally, it made for spectacular arguments, but for the most part their puzzle pieces slid into a natural and effortless place.

One of these arguments took place just a few weeks before the night of the party. Aunt Biola was so talented she could have pulled any number of hustles. Because of her braiding skills, she was our community hairdresser. She was also a seamstress on the side. Topping all, though, was the fact that Aunt Biola was an immaculate cook. In fact, she had been trained at culinary school. Whenever the West Africans of Alberta got together, she would produce a breathtaking table of dishes, mixing African and European traditions with panache, the sheer number of dishes requiring side tables and the kids' card table all jammed into their small dining room. At these events, everyone would chip in some dish or other, but Aunt Biola's *Salone Salad* or *pɛpɛsup* with *ɔgfut* or with *krenkre* would outdo all else, dominating the table in size and opulence. Aunty Biola was also the best at rejigging Sierra Leonean meals into new, Canadian contexts. She was the one who would discover a unique substitute for palm oil or cassava leaves, when everyone else was making do with tomato paste or spinach.

One day, Aunty Biola surprised everyone by getting a job. It was a cooking job that started very early in the morning and ended early in the afternoon, so she would be home with plenty of time to have Uncle's food waiting on the table. Yet no one was surprised more by her shift into the world of the duly employed than Uncle Biola. He simply had not seen it coming. Truthfully, Uncle Biola is the kind of guy who only expects the world to go as he expects. Much as I'd love to frame his eccentricities — wearing summer clothes in winter, shouting as his default volume — as some form of heroics, in fact, he is simply a man who does not see the point of yet another perspective when his own will do just fine. Part of why he doesn't feel the need to think beyond the next thirty seconds is that there is nothing in his world to predict. Anticipation is the activity of the weak or needy, or of pointless dreamers. I don't know this for sure, but it seems to me that one of the reasons why he married my aunt is that her sense of order and meticulous planning produced solidly reliable routines in my uncle's life. And perhaps this bubble of predictability she produced for him also created certain illusions for him: that he was in control of world's events; that inevitabilities were a natural function of gravity or the law of physics; that the woman he married, who ensured his clothes were ironed and his belly filled, would always be that same woman who ensured he was properly clothed and fed. That supper would always be placed in front of him at 6:00 p.m.

"It *will* be placed in front of you at 6:00 p.m.," my aunt protested. But Uncle Biola was still too much in shock to process her words. It had never occurred to him that he might have a wife who would elicit some measure of satisfaction outside of the house in a capacity that had nothing to do with him. It so defied his expectations that he had nothing to say. He just retreated into himself — in that way I saw him do at the party, when I glimpsed him as a "real" African man — his eyes cagey and red, his chest rising and falling in silence.

Later that night they had an intense fight that was defined by the acrid silences they launched at each other. My aunt called my mom, her voice rising and rising in pitch, just starting to crack. Another uncle of mine, Mark — who we called Modu — called Uncle Biola and tried to reason with him. Uncle Modu was a university professor and reasoned everything out. His eyes had a piercing intensity, but his belly and his laughter were both soft. When I think of Uncle Modu, I can't imagine any other version of him living in Sierra Leone. He was younger than my parents' generation by about ten years, and he left Sierra Leone about ten years after them. To me, this made him a very recent arrival, but somehow he was already more Canadian than all of them. He adapted to the food; winter annoyed but didn't exasperate him; he spoke French. It made me wonder if there was really no such thing as a "real" African man, no alternate universe that I was being deprived of. Maybe, if ever there was an alternate universe, we were already living in it: West Africans on the Prairies, transforming and being transformed by simply being there. Of all my displaced relatives,

Uncle Modu was the least likely to refer back to their lives in Sierra Leone as a touchstone for recuperation or sense-making in Canada. He was a great storyteller and often recalled extraordinary-sounding events to me about life in Freetown, but these stories – his old life – were just an aspect of his totality, the foundational layer of an ever-accreting life. If Uncle Biola was lodged in the present, devoid of expectations from a sheer lack of imagination, Uncle Modu was always reconsidering the future, imagining newer and newer possibilities.

"Eh, *bo*," he cajoled Uncle Biola. "Let's not make a to-do here. *Trɛnkman nɔ fɔ fɛn plaba.*"

Uncle Biola glared at him, his breath stirring from somewhere deep in his chest. But my soft-bellied professor of an uncle did not relent. He let out his sigh.

"*Bo*," he insisted softly.

The following week everyone was over at our place celebrating Aunty Biola's success at landing her job. Uncle Biola seemed to have overcome his surprise, though there was something extra to his energy that night. Although he was laughing in high spirits, occasionally I would see my mom give my dad a wary look. In fact, thinking back, everyone seemed vaguely cautious around Uncle Biola that night. The only people who seemed insensible were Paul and Mary, our token Africans who were from the Caribbean. Paul was the incessant joker of the group. Every single sentence he uttered would raise raucous laughter or loud groans. His wife, Mary, was very thin, light-skinned, and considerably taller than him. Paul was a compact, arrow-headed man with darting eyes.

He often held his hands in a pose of expectant reverence, his fingertips just touching as though he were on the verge of postulating or professing something profound. Unlike Uncle Modu who *was* a professor, everything about Paul seemed to aspire toward academic authority. His constant ribbing was the generous contrast to this persona that nobody took seriously anyway. I liked Paul because he was one of the few adults who seemed to give as much attention to the kids as to everyone else. I never understood his jokes, but I felt included whenever he launched one into the general revelry. Sometimes, he had hardly finished the joke before I was barking out in gleeful appreciation. Often, I laughed even louder when the surrounding response seemed sluggish. I felt protective of his sense of humour. At times it was only me and Mary – who without fail tittered silently at every single one of his jokes, her shoulders bouncing up and down – who reflected Paul's merriment back at him. On this night, Paul's joking seemed to punctuate the tension around Uncle Biola's energy. Although the two seemed to reflect jubilance at each other, in truth there was something very precise in each one's delivery that completely missed the other's. It was as though they were funhouse mirrors to each other, reflecting approximations.

I didn't really pick up on it, though. All of my participatory laughter was masking an inner turmoil. A few days earlier, I had careened between feeling invincible and feeling vulnerable, and I was still struggling to reconcile the feeling. I kept pressing my hand to the logo on the chest of my shirt, like a talisman of protection. But instead, my hand felt jolted by the hammering heart beneath it. I was wearing a brand-new Polo shirt. It was a light pink, a hue approaching what we used to think of as *Miami Vice* pink. I wish I didn't need to, but I feel compelled to explain that *Miami Vice* was a hit police drama in the eighties (Don Johnson's break-out show) that managed to capture our attention as much for the striking neon fashion it displayed as for its narrative-thin, action-packed storylines. My shirt hinted at that brand of pink, and so would be noticeable to anyone of my generation, but it had a softer, more conciliatory tone. The logo featured a horse-mounted polo player brandishing his mallet. It was iconic. I loved this man and his mallet. I loved the purity of the icon. My mom was forever buying me watered-down brand look-alikes: Lee jeans instead of Levi's, Sanyo portable cassette players instead of Sony Walkman, Janzy backpacks instead of JanSport. This was my first Polo shirt – not Pollo or Po-lo or Pillo but *Polo* – and the heat of its logo against my chest filled me with a sense of power. I knew it would get a reaction from my cousins. It did. Even Paul gave me a knowing wink. I was invincible.

When my friend Gabriel walked out of the store, cold and self-certain, with four bottles of Polo cologne in his bag, he taught me a new way of accurately understanding myself in the eyes of Albertans. If he was unmolested because he understood himself to be an unmolestable creature, then surely I would be unseen because I knew myself to be an unseeable creature. What Gabriel didn't teach me, though, was how to *feel* invincible. I was so inspired by this new vision of myself he had helped me toward that I didn't stop to think about how I felt about this transformed self. I think there must have been some part of me that was torn about it. I remember going back to that very same store that Gabriel had pillaged the day before, determined to reproduce his feat. I kept my gaze away from the surly, pock-faced stockboy who was barely older than me. He had tried to flip up the collar of his Lacoste shirt, but one side remained flopped inward, almost drooping to his collar bone. I scoffed to myself. I admit: I felt a measure of confidence. But it was not the usual type of confidence. It was the confidence that comes with recognizing a new concept. When certain pathways in our brain connect, we feel good. I think this is even more powerfully felt when the new concept aligns with an old mystery, something that we've experienced or encountered regularly throughout our lives but lacked the knowledge of or language for to the extent that it remained opaque, unnameable. Gabriel's cool indifference was the connector for me. It sparked a trail of recognition that wriggled through my brain, lighting up dark avenues that I had suspected were there but couldn't find my way through. And when two pathways intersected, my whole mind lit up with a dopamine dose of disillusionment that was irresistible. *This* is what I felt. I was high on understanding.

But as I stood in the drugstore aisle, staring at those bottles of Polo, I couldn't maintain the feeling. I still felt unseen, but not in the clear, dopamine-doused way that I had earlier. Maybe I was an unseeable creature. Maybe not. I was certainly a creature of some sort, a confounding, numinous sort of creature. But was that enough to protect me? All of this ruminating interfered with my feelings of invincibility. I knew I had to act quickly or I would draw attention to myself and the whole thing would blow up in my face. I had been standing, frozen in thought in the aisle, for too long as it was. The stockboy huffed past me, flicking at his collar. I made my decision. I picked up a box of Polo and dropped it into my backpack. I swung the bag over my shoulder and walked toward the door. I had deliberately taken the box while the pock-faced, drooping-collared stockboy was walking away from me, but still in the aisle. It seemed to confirm my particular brand of invisibility, especially when he got to the end of the aisle and quickly disappeared around the corner without a glance backward. I made my way down the aisle and toward the exit. Out of the corner of my eye I could make out several employees huddled at a till, but I ignored them. If my theory was right, I would be unseen to them because I am unseeable in this country. I knew that in the simplest terms I did not count. That is why people were not satisfied when I continually responded *here* when they persisted, no, where are you *really* from? Coming out of my mouth, where I am *really* from (here) doesn't count. That is why I had virtually no academic teachers encourage me when I was young, despite (I now recognize) my clearly academic bent. My intellect didn't count. That is why nobody saw any point in recognizing Black History Month in Alberta until 2017 — more than two centuries into the Prairies' Black history. Our presence here doesn't count. My theory was that these were the proof of my invincibility and, like Gabriel, who understood how to take advantage of his position in the world with brilliant clarity, I only had to fill the role that was expected of me to get the things I wanted.

The trouble was, my theory was not right. Or, I should say it was incomplete. As I neared the door, I had to pass directly past the huddle of young workers, and I couldn't help myself: I glanced toward them as I made my exit. They were all bent over some task on the counter – I think it was a magazine – except for one of them. He was standing erect, serenely surveying. Now his collar was inexplicably and perfectly flipped up, as though on alert, as though sensing something amiss. In the millisecond of my glance, it seemed, too, that his acne disaster had vanished. His hair, which I had never noticed before, had a Tom Cruise shag à la *Risky Business*. What I had taken earlier as surliness now read as low-grade disdain. Frankly, he looked cool. He stood calmly, his oblivious coworkers chattering beneath him, sunlight from the store window shining on his face, his eyes falling on my backpack with calm inner understanding. If not for the darkness of his hair and his peaceful demeanour, he would have reminded me completely of Gabriel. I looked away as quickly as I could have. Something in me did not want to see anything in him as remotely close to Gabriel. But I'm sure in my hastiness I must have looked furtive and just added to the guilt I was slowly projecting from my orbit.

"Hey," I heard him call. I ignored it. *Don't slow down*, I warned myself. *Don't look back*, I urged. I felt myself slow my pace. *What are you doing*? *You idiot, keep going*! I did not keep going. I turned to face him, like a wildebeest who knows he will not make it across the river, who can only imagine the crocodile's jaws around his neck, who perhaps welcomes the end of the flight and the oncoming darkness instead. When I faced him, I did not see the jaws of a crocodile. His eyes seemed vaguely unfocused, as though he was looking right through me. Confused, I glanced behind me but there was no one else. He pointed at me — or what felt like through me — and said, "Your backpack." I stood frozen, feeling the crocodile's jaws tighten against my throbbing Adam's apple. "JanSport," he said and flipped a thumb skyward. Then it clicked. He was approving of my backpack. I hated that bag and I usually tucked it under my seat or flipped it face down or otherwise tried to hide the fact that it was a ridiculous look-alike that my mom had bought for me, not caring or knowing the difference between the trendy JanSport and the no-name Janzy or Janzen or whatever it was called. Even the logo was a shameless imitation of the original brand, which was a smart looking dark blue patch with red lettering highlighted in white. It was unmistakably JanSport's brand. But the Janzy version was an off-colour patch and the letters had no highlights. It might fool an adult, or someone from a distance, but it would never pass muster if given a second investigation by someone in the know. And in my circles, *everyone* was in the know. But somehow, whether because of the distance or the fact that he wasn't really that cool after all, the surly-faced boy with the indecisive collar did *not* give it the twice-over. He seemed to think I was in possession of the genuine article. I let him. For all that I thought I had been identified, he had not actually seen me. Just like that I eased back into my familiar invisibility. I slipped out of the store. The world ambled by.

But my theory of unseeability was only partially complete. I was unseen for the most part, but that depended on the context.

So, while my academic educators hardly noticed me – except for when I didn't turn in assignments or did poorly on exams – I was regularly seen by gym teachers, basketball coaches, track and field trainers, and the like. Often, these characters would hunt me down in the first week of school and urge me to sign up for tryouts without knowing anything (else) about me. Also, I was seen by everyone whenever I did anything funny. And I often tried to do something funny, since, who doesn't like being the centre of attention? And it was clear that the role of slapstick comic was generally approved of. This was the era in which Eddie Murphy was breaking out in *Saturday Night Live*. He had not yet achieved the watershed moment that *Delirious* heralded, an utter transformation of how comedy could be delivered, particularly by Black men – witty, brazen, racially defiant. It took Richard Pryor's cutting critiques to a completely new level. Before that, though, he was often struggling to reinvent characters like Buckwheat and Gumby, whose comedy was propelled as much by costumes as by words, engaging in a tug of war between slapstick and something else. Before Eddie Murphy broke that mould, a Black man who *acted* funny was a seeable creature when I was young. And, therefore, so was I. I remember a friend of mine, who *was* witty, observed that people liked my style of joking because it had nothing to say. At the time I was insulted. Now I marvel at how astute he was at such a young age. But the one way in which I was most consistently seen, especially when I was out in public by myself, was as a potential law-breaker. It was common for rough-looking white men to approach me at the train station and offer to sell me drugs. I grew familiar with the watchful eye of the police if I was walking by a cruiser or happened to be nearby some officers for some reason or other. In retail stores, this translated into plainclothes security guards following me through the shop. It seems silly to only recognize it today, but the one context in which the test of my unseeability was most likely to fail was if I engaged as a shoplifter.

Not only did I *not* recognize this at the time, I doubled down. As soon as I made it out of the drugstore with my loot in my bag, I got it in my head to go into the very next store – Eaton's downtown – and do it again. This, I think occurred to me in part because, unlike Gabriel, I had not been able to sweep four bottles of cologne into my bag. I had planned to do so and even as I was reaching for the bottles, I had it in my mind to replicate Gabriel's feat. But, as I pointed out, I was not feeling the purity of cool indifference that Gabriel displayed. I was struggling between the two feelings that my sense of being unseen evoked in me: invincibility and vulnerability. Without realizing it, I reconciled the two feelings by taking no more risks than one bottle of Polo. Now, as I strode down the street, the world blind to my presence, I overwhelmingly felt like I needed to make up for my earlier doubt. The instant I saw Eaton's in front of me, I turned into the department store with no plan or inclination of what I was going to do exactly. When I saw the Polo shirt and its hinting *Miami Vice* pink, I didn't even hesitate. I plucked it from the rack and swept it into my Janzy bag. As I walked out of the store, I felt a wave of vindication come over me. It was as though the situation had resolved itself by beckoning to me. I had had no plan, and then, suddenly, the shirt had appeared in front of me, the solution to every Janzy problem my unwitting parents had foisted on me. I saw the horseman, his mallet in full swing. I knew nothing of the sport of polo. The polo player, too, was strangely anonymous to me, ubiquitously recognizable, but lacking any personal biography. I had only the vaguest sense that the logo was meant to hint at something aspirational, something classy. I saw in it something purely physical. The man on the horse, his mallet held up in mid-gesture, the frozen movement. It felt like pure power to me. Of course it did. Even then, I had a sense of the enticing power of horses. Although in my childhood experience it was mainly girls who drew them and fawned over them, it was impossible even for me – especially in this part of the West – not to recognize their status as brokers of power. They were everywhere in our modern society, especially in Cowtown. We had the Stampede after all, a massive ten-day long indulgence of rodeo culture (with a healthy injection of commercial shine). And though girls, primarily, doted over horses, the boys around me also had their version of pining in the form of horsepower. They noted it in all of the hyper-masculine vehicles that dotted our pop culture landscape – from Delorians in *Back to the Future*, to Ferraris in *Magnum P.I.*, or TransAms in *Knight Rider*. I could recognize the horse in the Polo logo as a basic unit in all of this fawning. Maybe, too, there was something familiar in the arc of the mallet swing. I had encountered many stories distilled through African and African American culture when I was growing up. For example, some of the Brer Rabbit stories had counterparts in Krio folklore. I was very attuned to these kinds of folk stories, possibly in an inchoate yearning for some sort of connection between the two continents that collided inside me. So, I was aware of the mythical figure of John Henry, though I didn't fully know who he was or the details of his story. I knew it had something to do with his strength and an impressive swing of his hammer or a mallet. I don't know for certain today, but I feel there was some unconscious affinity in me for this potential congruity: the physicality and the anonymity of the Polo logo, its action frozen in time, the rider stripped of identity, and the image of John Henry, a figure of pure physicality, whose gesture of strength was a mirroring swing of his mallet, but beyond that was someone whose identity was utterly beyond my grasp.

At this point, I had walked out of the store and had turned down the street when I felt a hand on my shoulder. I didn't hesitate; I didn't turn around. I burst into a run at speeds worthy of any starry-eyed track coach from my past. But the hand had gripped my Janzy firmly and with the force of my forward momentum it was coming off my shoulder. I couldn't run. I half turned, the bag slipping off of my shoulder, and gave it an enormous tug. Now I was facing my assailant, a skinny man who I had noticed near the door when I walked in, but who I hadn't given a second thought to, so immersed was I in my sense of unseeability. I knew that if I ran away, he wouldn't be able to catch me. I was — despite my reluctance to satisfy every track coach's stereotypical view of me — very athletic. Every year I qualified for the Provincials in the sprinting events. I had a small collection of medals and ribbons on my bookcase in my room. I could have dropped the bag and flown. But I was worried about identifying objects. As it was,

I was wearing a football jacket from the school I attended. Maybe this plainclothes security guard was not as familiar with the local school colours as I thought, but I didn't know. I also worried about any contents in my Janzy that might be able to identify me. For the most part, I was pretty sure my bag was empty except for a hoodie, a couple of library books, and of course, the bottle of Polo with the shirt to match. But I wasn't 100% sure and didn't want to risk it. A tug of war ensued. The security guard was shouting at me, raising a ruckus. I sensed people approaching. I was getting desperate. I gave the Janzy a mad yank. The security guard let out a grunt and the bag lurched out of my grasp. The cheap zipper had broken and the Janzy's contents had spilled out onto the street. I snatched what I could – only my hoodie – and leapt away, sprinting blindly, breathlessly. I had walked into Eaton's feeling invincibly unseeable, but as I pounded my way through the streets, my only thought was to get away from all of those greedy eyes plastered to my back.

I don't know how long I ran, but probably the guard had given up long before I stopped. Eventually, I realized no one was chasing me and I could stand for a moment, hunched over, catching my breath. That's when I noticed a flash of pink buried in the handful of hoodie I was gripping. I stared at it, my mind still spinning as I gulped for more oxygen. I had run a huge distance, zigzagging through alleyways and randomly changing direction. At one point, I had dashed straight through City Hall, terrified to be in the bosom of so much scrutinizing power and simultaneously awed by my own audacity at such a move. I finally came to a rest just outside, wheezing with my hand against the building's wall.

Little did I know, but I had run straight down a road of Black history. A century earlier the Lewis family had lived in a log cabin on Stephen Avenue. John Ware's daughter Nettie was born there and describes it as being directly across the street from the Queen's Hotel.[52] This hotel was demolished in 1982 to make way for the modern expansion to City Hall. The municipal building still stands there today and was brand new when I was sagged against its side, catching my breath as a teenage fugitive.

In the 1890s Stephen Avenue, still important today, was essentially Calgary's Main Street. In my flight through City Hall's public atrium — I might suggest — I had effectively travelled along the city's historic spine. I had walked through a Black historical space that I could have claimed had I known about it. Then again, what space of history *would* I be claiming? John Ware hated Calgary. He was a cattleman, not a city man; moreover, the city was not kind to him. He often faced the worst kind of racism when he was here. From time to time John had to be in the city for supplies or work or some necessity; otherwise, he avoided it. As soon as he could, John established himself in the grasslands to the south, where he started his first ranch near Millarville. But one quirky Calgary story stands out to me. The story goes that John was bringing cattle to Calgary, but there had been a flood and a bridge along the way was out. According to the tall tale, the legendary cowboy was able to coax his herd into the waters and under his gentle guidance they

52 Velma Carter and Wanda Leffler Akili, *The Window Of Our Memories* (St. Albert, AB: Black Cultural Research Society of Alberta, 1981), 85.

were so assured he could step calmly across their backs – a living, bovine bridge – as they made their way to the other side. Though fanciful, this story has always struck me as a powerful retelling of how people viewed Ware's skills. Other than Martin Luther King, I can't think of another Black person whose legend flirts with the impact of Jesus Christ (in this case, walking on water). It turns out, however, that this story, as dramatic as it sounds, is an impossibility. It never happened. Instead, it is an unconscious fabrication of my mind. When I finally researched specific sources to nail down the tale's details for this book, I discovered my error. I have carried so many stories about John Ware in my head that over the years several details of his life seem to have coalesced into this fantastic tale. Here are the facts: he was known to have crossed a bridge at Calgary after walking his cattle through the city when it was illegal to do so. During an outbreak of mange he fell into a vat of brine while helping cattle into the vat. Most tellingly, there were often tributes made to Ware's physical size, often including his ability to step over calves. These references have influenced stories – readily available today – about him walking on or over fully grown cattle.[53]

---

53 "Meet John Ware — Legendary Black Cowboy," *Secret Life of Canada*, produced by CBC Podcasts, 5 February 2019, https://www.cbc.ca/radio/secretlifeofcanada/meet-john-ware-legendary-black-cowboy-1.5006879. ¶ Tyler Dixon, "Legendary Cowboy," *Calgary Guardian*, May 19, 2016, https://calgaryguardian.com/legendary-cowboy/. ¶ Historica Canada Teacher Community, "John Ware," *Historica Canada Education Portal*, accessed 15 December 2025, http://education.historicacanada.ca/en/tools/155. ¶ Craig Baird, "Rancher John Ware," *Canadian History Ehx*, 20 January 2020, https://canadaehx.com/2020/01/20/rancher-john-ware/.

This stew of storymaking, coupled with my archival neglect — and spiced up with a dash of some Christ-like aspirations I apparently have for Ware — resulted in this fantastic tale.

The story has some use, though. When I think of it today, I try to imagine what my teenage self would make of John Ware and his many legendary feats. When I was that age, I often felt like I was walking just off-balance, on the wrong side of gravity, always struggling against or with some mysterious inertia that didn't seem to affect anyone else. It would have blown my mind to know that I had just passed through the former home of the family of a revered Black man, as though I were the ghost of some distant, unborn past. It would have made me feel more solid to know that I was not the only one trying to master this balancing act. Later in life, long after I knew about the Wares and the Lewises and the many Black ranchers and cowhands that populated the Prairies, I stumbled across another, completely different kind of ghost. In Ethiopia, there is an ethnic group known as the Hamar who are nomadic cowherders. In a demonstration of how central cattle are to their lives, the Hamar have a tradition that all young boys must undergo as a rite of passage. *Ukuli Bula* is their tradition of bull jumping and requires every boy to leap onto the back of a bull and then continue walking across the backs of several more in a show of aptitude and bravery. I've watched some examples on YouTube (because . . . YouTube) and the rite sounds more difficult than it looks. To be sure, it is challenging. But the whole process is helped by the participation of the community. Women sing and dance in enthusiastic encouragement. The bulls are lined up side by side and held in place by other community members. It is not usually more than four or five bulls that the boys must cross, each bull representing a single step of their journey. I was struck by the group effort involved. Although it is meant to be a rite of passage for specific boys to cross a threshold into manhood, the entire tradition is supported by everyone, the boy wrapped in the spirit of community love.

Now, I can imagine John Ware stepping gracefully from cow to cow, each step a reassuring demonstration of his newfound footing in this far-flung cattle kingdom of Western Canada. Although he seems to walk alone, he, too, like the Hamar boys, is surrounded by a loving community that informs his sure steps, even as those steps guide the tentative cattle beneath him.

FIG 32 This Hamar youth treads an Afrofuturistic trail for John Ware and me to follow. Photo by Bharat Patel.

It feels as though there is still something of Africa echoing in that gesture of unusual crossings. I knew nothing of it as a teenage thief, exhausted by flight. My body was hunched over, one arm propped against my knee, one arm outstretched against City Hall — the building that had covered over the historic dwelling of one of the most meaningful families in all of the Prairies' Black history. That echo bounces inside me, across time and space, from the Hamar to John Ware to me. Some estimate that the Ethiopian tradition is several thousand years old, but it is still alive and thriving. Its vitality fuels the poetry of my imagination, showing me that the ghosts of Black history can still haunt here, can possess a gesture, can collapse time, can linger in the corners of memory's oblivion. Somehow, I was both a ghost and a victim of that ghost. Somehow, I was alone in the city and completely surrounded by a buried history. One day, I would learn to see that buried history everywhere, supporting me, guiding my steps, singing and dancing my name in enthusiastic encouragement.

A few nights later, I ironed out that crumpled, pink shirt and wore it to Aunt Biola's party like a warrior's sacred armour: Heracles's holy skin, crafted by the great god Hephaestus himself. The logo of the anonymous horseman swinging his mallet shone out like stardust twinkling from my cosmic source material. I felt powerful and seen in that shirt. I felt I had earned that power through the many trials that eventually led to me wearing that shirt — some of my own doing, some not. And it did get the desired effect: my cousins were all obligingly admiring. The fact that even Paul seemed to recognize something valuable in my outfit, even though he may not have been as versed in the language of brands as young people were, only added to the power I felt. All through the night, I felt the logo against my breast, burning with its own undeniable potency.

THE PARTY

Somewhere around eleven o'clock in the evening, the party my parents were throwing for my Aunt Biola hit its euphoric high: King Sunny Ade boomed out; the Africans pounced onto the dance floor like Olympic athletes, everyone chasing a medal, everyone confident in their ability to win a medal, everyone glorying in the rhythm of summer that pulsed through these Games.

Everyone except for my Aunt Biola. She had been quiet most of the night, only dancing intermittently. She had a watchful, guarded look, especially when Uncle Biola took centre stage, drawing in the evening's energy, spinning toward some undefined edge. Her approach to her husband's careless predilections for public joy over his own physical health had always been no-nonsense, exacting even, like a school Marm or a prison warden. But on this night when she was being celebrated, there was a subtly subdued cast to her. Unlike Uncle Biola, she was a person who generally avoided being the centre of attention. But that had never stopped her from joining in with celebrations like this one. At the time, I could only put her hesitancy down to something particularly reckless in Uncle Biola's disregard to consequences of any kind:

the party-goers' veiled apprehension, his precarious health, his wife's feelings. On the other hand, Aunt Biola did at times seem over-vigilant when it came to his health. Certainly my uncle saw it that way, and her attitude to *that* was undeniably disproving. She would criticize him full of irritation bordering on eye-rolling indignation. But once, he suffered a hypoglycemic episode when he had been drinking and dancing too much and actually collapsed. I remember seeing Aunt Biola push her face almost up against his, shouting his name over and over again, her usual tone of annoyance drenched in a desperation I had never heard before. It made my heart well in terror. He recovered and she was furious with him for weeks. But the event showed me that for all of her sterile disappointments in him, a more powerful feeling was beating just beneath the surface.

Perhaps this is why I didn't feel any concern over her glowering look when Uncle Biola's state suddenly teetered toward the "real" African man I hungrily yearned to see. If anything, I felt protective of him and dismissive of her critical stance. In some ways, I was absorbing the rules of a particular African masculinity that was intermittently on view for me. I was far more prepared to think that she was haranguing him unnecessarily than I was prepared to acknowledge he was dismissing her unfairly. And when my parents joined her side to entreat him, I felt disappointed. I didn't want their intervention. I didn't want any of them to interfere: my parents with their avuncular concern, my Uncle Modu's soft-bellied reasoning, Paul and Mary's side-eyed cajoling. They were being careful, caring even, but at that moment I hated them.

I hated their impulse to sugar-coat, to temper Uncle Biola, to fetter his intrinsic energy. I felt that it belittled him. I felt that he was likely belittled regularly by Canadians who did not understand him or the value of his particular energy. I had played a role in the belittling myself by yearning for someone else's accent to come out of his mouth, someone urbane and silver-tongued, someone white. Likely, it was my guilt as much as my sense of protectiveness over my Uncle Biola's uncompromising "Africanness" that jolted me into speaking.

"No," I said, putting a hand on his shoulder. "Uncle Biola is right."

The room of onlookers paused, confused by my statement. To be clear, Uncle Biola hadn't even said anything. There was nothing for me to be refuting ("no") or supporting ("Uncle Biola is right") at all. My words were simply inserted as nonsense within an already tense atmosphere looking for an excuse to either deflate or explode. My parents turned to me with an exasperated look. Uncle Modu scratched his head. My words hung in the air between us. *Uncle Biola is right.* Mary gave a resigned shrug, but for the first time I had ever seen Paul had a reproachful look on his face, almost irritated. Increasingly, it appeared that my words, meant to come to my uncle's rescue, had added an air of vulnerability to the night's ambience. Suddenly, I was the one adrift from the rest, unsure and isolated; I was the one who needed rescuing. As a matter of fact, Uncle Biola's look was probably most disconcerting of all. His red eyes had focused narrowly on me. His lip was not quite curled in a snarl. He had the distinct look on his face that

I was an unwanted thing: a stain, or a bad odour. I lost what little composure I had as a twelve-year-old. I was reminded of how this generation of Sierra Leonean's – my parents' generation – had been raised to see children as an inferior species, something whose value is only measured in report card grades and school recitals. Otherwise, children had no business inserting themselves in the concerns of adults. Too, this was the early 1980s, and in that era it was not uncommon to punish children physically at one's whim, even if everyone didn't agree with it. The possibility was a legitimate one. This was even more the case with immigrants from West Africa. They had no hesitancy over "knocking sense" into a child or "setting them proper."

At this point, I wanted to slink away unseen. But there was no escaping this moment. I had stepped right into it and now I had to face those consequences. My uncle let out a low growl. From the depths of his volcanic belly he rumbled my name and it was full of heat, full of molten potential:

"Bat."

I closed my eyes, waiting for the physical punishment to descend. I only had enough time to wonder what my parents would feel, what they would do, when Uncle Biola rained his punishment down on me. Surely they would intervene? But, honestly, I wasn't sure they would. It was part of the code they grew up with: any family member can discipline a child of that family. All of the adults were considered parents to us. It's a cliché, yes, but the saying that it takes a village was an actual lived experience for me. From my teen perspective, this was its dark side.

Then I felt a hand land gently on my knee.

"No."

I opened my eyes. My Aunty Biola was glaring fiercely at her husband, one hand protectively held to my knee.

"Do not even think about it," she hissed at him.

I was too stunned to know what to think. Too many layers of possibilities seemed to be draping over me, burying me beneath. I was defending *him*. Now, because of that, she was defending *me*. In the background, the music was still pumping loudly. Jimmy Cliff belted out "Wonderful World, Beautiful People" in his glorious, soaring voice, the cellos shuddering in refrain. I was confused and ashamed and angry and annoyed. My mother sat down on my other side, between me and Uncle Biola. My dad wrapped an arm around Uncle Biola's shoulder. We sat in silence, enfolding each other in our various gestures of protectiveness, our conflicted intensities of love.

"Eh *bo*, can't we dance now?"

It was Paul. Our Caribbean friend had feigned an African accent when he stressed *bo*. But in deploying the term, even clumsily, he had also shown how he, too, was one of the family, trying to worm his way in from the outside. It was too much: everyone burst out laughing and I found myself joining them. For once, I was in on the joke.

Later, in the kitchen with my Aunt Biola, I apologized for causing a scene. She looked at me serenely with that same unusual intensity she had been aiming at me all evening long.

"If I didn't know better, I'd say you were trying to steal my thunder." I didn't know what to say. I shook my head. She smiled at me and turned to pull something out from under the kitchen table. "I have been keeping something for you."

It was my Janzy. I stared at it in shock while she placed it in my hands. Again, I was speechless. Was this some sort of set-up? Were my parents now going to jump out of the cupboards and demand to know everything? I was mortified and desperate. How did she get this bag? Was it even mine? My hand fumbled over the zipper. It zipped up and down flawlessly. There were two library books in it, the ones I had borrowed. There was no sign of the Polo cologne.

"I fixed the zipper for you," said my aunt, the part-time seamstress.

I felt something waver inside me. It slowly dawned on me what she was doing. From the living room, the music cranked up another notch. I heard loud laughter and could make out my father's solemn bass rollicking beneath the music. Despite the tensions of the evening, everybody sounded happy. They were happy. They were happy for Aunt Biola. I, too, was happy for Aunt Biola, the woman who unhesitatingly came to my defence. But I kept forgetting that she was the whole reason for this party. I knew that she had recently got a job, but I didn't know much more. I didn't know how getting a job had forced my uncle's insides into ambitious wrestling moves. I didn't know that we were in a difficult economy and that my uncle had been laid off. I didn't know that my aunt had never had a chance to practice her cooking and managerial skills in a professional setting. I didn't know that most restaurants were cutting back in this economic period, nor that only restaurants attached to another business, like a retail store, were in a position to hire. I certainly didn't know that department stores were hesitant to hire Black people, even in the eighties, and that Aunt Biola never thought she would get the job when she first read the ad for a cook at the Eaton's Tea Room. But she did. She got that job and, as she was walking out of the building, she was in a perfect position to see the altercation taking place between an in-store security guard and a young man, just a boy, really, who looked *exactly* like her increasingly furtive-eyed nephew, who used to be so full of outward facing energy not so long ago.

I didn't know any of this yet. But standing in my kitchen, feeling confused and ashamed, it was becoming clearer to me what my aunt was doing. She gave me a long look and a quick hug. For the briefest moment, I felt that logo on my breast being pressed into my skin, burning between our beating hearts. When she returned to the room full of musicked revellers, drunk on joy, I heard a loud cheer and the Mighty Sparrow rhythmed out yet another notch louder.

This is what my aunt was doing: when she gave me that quick hug, she whispered in my ear, "Tomorrow." In the wholeness of the gesture, I felt my flattened identity uncrumple and fill out. There would be pain to come, undoubtedly. And shame. And tears. But even as I knew that, I never doubted the love I was being enveloped in, that we were all entwined in. West Africans on the Prairie. Black cowboys on the savannah. My aunt was giving me the gift of our brand of double-yoked love. It is the love that promises pain and shame and tears tomorrow. But more importantly, it promises tomorrow. She had spelled it out for me for the rest of my life: between the trails of our Black Prairies and our African legacies, there is history, there are cowboys, and because there is love, there is always a tomorrow.

ACKNOWLEDGEMENTS

First, I would like to thank the Athabasca University Writer in Residence program for gifting me the time and the mental space to focus on writing for a year. In this regard I want especially to thank Angie Abdou and Paul Huebener. Thanks, too, to the rest of the writer in residence committee, Manijeh Mannani, and the Faculty of Humanities and Social Sciences Talks committee.

A big thanks to Peter Midgley, my editor. Peter you were the perfect editor for this book. You know your CMOS from your OED, your Dutch East India from your British East India Companies, and your Mighty Sparrow from your Black Uhuru. Who else could have gathered the trailing threads of my wide-ranging thoughts together with such confidence and comfort? There has never ever been any doubt in mind: you are a "real" African man. Also, to the very capable production and promotions coordinator at AU Press, Karyn Wisselink, thank you for being so on top of every step of the book's production. Your work ethic is colossal.

Thanks to all of my OC Commie Colleagues, Brendan, Keith, Michele, Noah, and Whitney, who have always shown me support, encouragement, and forgiveness when I have been unable to give it to myself. Similarly, thanks to Kit Dobson and Uche Umezurike for timely support when things got tricky.

A special thanks to Cheryl Foggo, whose literary presence forms the ether of my creative output and whose writing always shows the paths away from anger. Thanks to my writing crew: Weyman, Teresa, Chimie, Tolu. I love our random interactions! Thanks to Lindsay Amundsen-Meyer for introducing me to stratigraphy and for showing such care toward the buried nature of buried histories. Thanks to Tammy Rosner, an enthusiastic researcher whose family knew Charles Dyson in Pincher Creek. Tammy is the one who cleared up the mystery of Dyson's double wedding for me. She has a wealth of information on both Charles Dyson and Liza Johnson (née Reed); watch out for her book, folks!

A very special thank you to Katrina H.B. Keefer at Trent University who very kindly guided me to "recaptive 7804" in the Liberated Africans Register for 1815 and gave me permission to use her screenshot. "Recaptive 7804" was a nineteen-year-old man whose name was Joze and who was branded with a "Crown and B" on his left breast. I wish I knew more about Joze than the paltry physical qualities noted in the Register, but I will be endlessly grateful for the work Dr. Keefer and her colleagues are doing to recover the histories of Africans whose humanity was mercilessly pulverized and scored over by the Atlantic slave trade. Do check out their research: https://languageofmarks.org/newHome/research.php

I would like to acknowledge Joze, a miraculous, impossible returnee; he is my symbolic ancestor and the prototype for Abiola.

I would like to give posthumous gratitude to John Bickersteth for his generosity and the honest warmth he extended to me. Little did I know at the time, but John had been the Bishop of Bath and

Wells, 1975–87. He was a confident and driven clergyman, but he was also a spontaneous and colourful man. He once preached peace to thousands of hippies at Glastonbury in the late seventies. Do check out his obituary in the *Church Times*, 16 March 2018.

The two poems that appear in this book, "Some Say. . ." and "A Black Hand Revisits," were originally published in *filling Station* 81 in 2023.

I must acknowledge the many Black cowboys and ranchers who acted as inspiration for me but did not make it into this text: Flora Wolfe, Lige Abel, Billy Welsh, Martha Proctor, and David Mills, to mention a few. This book would not have been possible without all of my historic collaborators, both those mentioned and unmentioned in the text.

Finally, a big thank you to the community of Prairie Africans I grew up with, who gave me so much, despite my reluctance, resistance, and straight-up ignorance. I especially thank my mum, who has always been the family historian for me, sharing stories, filling in the gaps, and encouraging connections. Thank you for reading and smoothing over my Krio cultural catastrophes in the text. Thank you, especially, for giving me the gift of an awkward upbringing.

LIST OF ILLUSTRATIONS

14 The Freeman Family. Statistics Canada fonds, R233-47-9-E, Census of the Prairie Provinces, 1916, District number 37, sub-district number 30, page 37, Library and Archives Canada. Image number 31228_4363980-00663, Library and Archives Canada, https://central.bac-lac.gc.ca/.redirect?app=census&id=42557885&lang=eng&ecopy=31228_4363980-00663

15 Freeman Family's Palimpsestic Blackness.

16 Family Brands, from left to right: Robert (V0T), Nettie (DC), William (Crazy 3 D), and John Ware (I9) (*North West Brand Book* 1900).

17 Walter Freeman's "Quarter Circle Reverse F Four" Brand (*Alberta Horse and Cattle Brands*, 1916–18).

18 Coat of Arms (52.125) granted to Robert Bickersteth in 1856.

19 Abiola Traces His Past. Katrina H. B. Keefer/Author.

20 Charles Dyson, "Bar One-Two" (*North West Brand Book*, 1900). Note, beneath is a brand owned by Pat Burns, one of the Calgary Stampede's Big Four founders.

21 My Path Through "Bar 1–2."

22 A Trace of Dyson's Bars.

23 The Running Iron's Way with Words.

24 The Jumping-Off Point of Brand Poetics.

25 M▯ne"

26 "I Lies Down."

27 "A Trace of the Truth."

28 The Poetics of Black Cattle Brands.

29 Two versions of "S Bar S" (*Alberta and Saskatchewan Brand Book*, 1907).

30 "Crazy P 7 Inverted Rafter," Eliza Dyson's brand (*Supplement to Alberta Horse and Cattle Brands*, 1914).

31 *Black Venus* (1957) by Margaret Burroughs (courtesy National Gallery of Art).

32 This Hamar youth treads an Afrofuturistic trail for John Ware and me to follow. Photo by Bharat Patel.

BIBLIOGRAPHY

"Meet John Ware — Legendary Black Cowboy." *Secret Life of Canada*, produced by CBC Podcasts, 5 February 2019. https://www.cbc.ca/radio/secretlifeofcanada/meet-john-ware-legendary-black-cowboy-1.5006879.

Adam, Karla. "A Crown Branded onto Bodies Links British Monarchy to Slave Trade." *Washington Post*. 27 September 2023. https://www.washingtonpost.com/world/2023/09/27/british-monarchy-slave-trade-brand/.

Baird, Craig. "Rancher John Ware." *Canadian History Ehx*. 20 January 2020. https://canadaehx.com/2020/01/20/rancher-john-ware/.

Baldwin, James. *No Name in the Street*. First Vintage International Edition. New York: Vintage Books, 2007.

Baldwin, James. *Nobody Knows My Name*. First Vintage International Edition. New York: Vintage Books, 1993.

Baldwin, James. *The Fire Next Time*. First Vintage International Edition. New York: Vintage Books, 1993.

Bickersteth, J. Burgon. *The Land of Open Doors: Being Letters from Western Canada, 1911–13*. Toronto: University of Toronto Press, 1976.

Black, Olivia. "Representations of Queer Cowboys in History, Literature, and Film." Bachelor's thesis, Providence College, 2025. https://digitalcommons.providence.edu/history_undergrad_theses/87/.

British Library, London. South Sea Company Archives. Additional Manuscripts. MS 2557, fo18r.

Carlos, Ann M., Jennifer Key, and Jill L. Dupree. "Learning and the Creation of Stock-Market Institutions: Evidence from the Royal African and Hudson's Bay Companies, 1670–1700." *Journal of Economic History* 58, no. 2 (June 1998): 318–344. https://doi.org/10.1017/S0022050700020532.

Carter, Velma, and Wanda Leffler Akili. *The Window Of Our Memories*. St. Albert, AB: Black Cultural Research Society of Alberta, 1981.

Centennial Book Committee F.W.U.A. High Prairie Local 204. *Pioneers Who Blazed the Trail: Local History of High Prairie, Alberta*. High Prairie, AB: Centennial Book Committee F.W.U.A. High Prairie Local 204, 1968.

Clarke, George Elliott. "Must All Blackness Be American?: Locating Canada in Borden's *Tightrope Time,* or Nationalizing Gilroy's *The Black Atlantic.*" In *Odysseys Home: Mapping African-Canadian Literature*, 73. Toronto: University of Toronto Press, 2002.

Dixon, Tyler. "Legendary Cowboy." *Calgary Guardian*. 19 May 2016. https://calgary guardian.com/legendary-cowboy/.

Donnan, Elizabeth, ed. *Documents Illustrative of the History of the Slave Trade to America*. Vol. 2, *The Eighteenth Century*. Washington, D.C.: Carnegie Institution of Washington, 1931.

Finney, Malcolm Awadajin. "Substratal Influence on the Morphosyntactic Properties of Krio." *Linguistic Discovery* 2, no. 2 (2004). https://doi.org/10.1349/PS1. 1537-0852.A.266.

Foran, Max, ed. *Grant MacEwan's Journals*. Edmonton, AB: Lone Pine, 1986.

Franke-Ruta, Garance. "How 'Washington' Became the Blackest Name in America." *The Atlantic*, 21 February 2011. https://www.theatlantic.com/politics/archive/ 2011/02/how-washington-became-the-blackest-name-in-america/71511/.

Fyle, Clifford N., and Eldred D. Jones. *A Krio–English Dictionary*. Oxford: Oxford University Press and Sierra Leone University Press, 1980.

Goldstein-Shirley, David. "Black Cowboys In the American West: A Historiographical Review." *Ethnic Studies Review* 20, no. 1 (1997): 79–89.

Grizzle, Stanley G. *My Name's Not George: The Story of the Brotherhood of Sleeping Car Porters*. Toronto: Umbrella Press, 1998.

Guan, Furui. "Chinese Cowboys: A Story of Resilience in the American Old West." Preprint, *ScienceOpen Preprints*, 25 July 2024, DOI: 10.14293/PR2199.000972.v1.

High Prairie & Area History Book Society. *Trails We Blazed Together: History of Grouard, High Prairie & Surrounding Areas*. High Prairie, AB: High Prairie & Area History Book Society, 1997.

High River Pioneer and Old Timers' Association. *Leaves from the Medicine Tree*. High River, AB: High River Pioneer and Old Timers' Association, 1960.

Historica Canada Teacher Community. "John Ware." Historica Canada Education Portal. Accessed 15 December 2025. http://education.historicacanada.ca/en/ tools/155.

hooks, bell. *Black Looks: Race and Representation*, 2 ed. New York: Routledge, 2015.

Hunt, Maria C. "'A History That's Been Suppressed': The Black Cowboy Story Is 200 Years Old." *The Guardian*, 19 May 2024, https://www.theguardian.com/ culture/ng-interactive/2024/may/19/black-cowboys-cowgirls-rodeos.

Ings, Frederick William. *Before the Fences: Tales from the Midway Ranch*. Nanton, AB: Nanton Historical Society, 1980.

Kersting, Dulce L. *Diversity on the Open Range: Exploring the Experiences of Minority Cowboys During the Nineteenth Century*. Jerry O'Neal Research Fellowship Report. Missoula, MT: Rocky Mountain Cooperative Ecosystem Studies Unit, 2011. https://files.cfc.umt.edu/cesu/NPS/UMT/2011/O'Neal_fellowship_Kersting_report.pdf.

Levenson, Jay A., Diogo Ramada Curto, and Jack C. Richard, eds. *Encompassing the Globe: Portugal and the World in the 16th & 17th Centuries*. Washington, D.C.: Arthur M. Sackler Gallery, Smithsonian Institution, 2007.

MacEwan, Grant. *John Ware's Cow Country*. Edmonton: Institute of Applied Art, Ltd., 1960.

Mather, Ken. *Frontier Cowboys and the Great Divide: Early Ranching in B.C. and Alberta*. Surrey, BC: Heritage House, 2013.

McKittrick, Katherine. *Demonic Grounds: Black Women and the Cartographies of Struggle*. Durham, NC: Duke University Press, 2006.

Morrison, Toni. *Beloved*. New York: Alfred A. Knopf, 2021.

Moten, Fred. *In the Break: The Aesthetics Of The Black Radical Tradition*. Minneapolis: University of Minnesota Press, 2003.

Mroz, Mike A. "Black Cowboys of the Cattle Frontier." *Legacy* 16, no. 1 (2016): 1–13. https://opensiuc.lib.siu.edu/legacy/vol16/iss1/3.

Porter, Kenneth W. "Negro Labor in the Western Cattle Industry, 1866–1900." *Labor History* 10, no. 3 (Summer 1969): 346–74.

Postma, Johannes. *The Dutch in the Atlantic Slave Trade, 1600–1815*. New York: Cambridge University Press, 1990.

Sharpe, Christina. *In the Wake: On Blackness and Being*. Durham, NC: Duke University Press, 2016.

Sierra Leone Public Archives. "Liberated African Department; Register Nos 7508–9758 [1815–1816]." British Library Endangered Archives Programme, EAP443/1/17/5. https://eap.bl.uk/archive-file/EAP443-1-17-5.

Sinclair, Niigaan. *Wînipêk: Visions of Canada from an Indigenous Centre*. Toronto: McLelland & Stewart, 2025.

Vernon, Karina. "The Black Prairies: History, Subjectivity, Writing." PhD diss., University of Victoria, 2008.

Voyages: The Trans-Atlantic Slave Trade Database. SlaveVoyages. https://www.slavevoyages.org/voyage/trans-atlantic#voyages.

Wai, Zubairu. *Epistemologies of African Conflicts: Violence, Evolutionism, and the War in Sierra Leone*. New York: Palgrave Macmillan, 2012.

Walls, Andrew F. "Crowther, Samuel Ajayi (A): Foremost African Christian of the Nineteenth Century." In *Dictionary of African Christian Biography*. Accessed 10 December 2025. https://dacb.org/stories/nigeria/legacy-crowther/.

Washington, Booker T. *Up from Slavery*. Oxford: Oxford University Press, 2000.

Whitman, T. Stephen. *The Price of Freedom: Slavery and Manumission in Baltimore and Early National Maryland*. New Haven, CT: Yale University Press, 1997.

Wynter, Sylvia. *On Being Human as Praxis*. Durham, NC: Duke University Press, 2015.

BRAND BOOKS

Alberta and Saskatchewan Brand Book. Edmonton [?]: n.p., 1907. https://archive.org/details/albertasaskatcheooalbe/mode/2up

Alberta Cattle and Horse Brands. Edmonton, J.W. Jeffrey, 1914.

Alberta Department of Agriculture. *Alberta Horse and Cattle Brands, 1915*. Edmonton: J.W. Jeffery, 1916. https://archive.org/details/albertahorsecattoounse_o/mode/2up.

Alberta Department of Agriculture. *Alberta Horse and Cattle Brands, 1916, 1917, 1918*. Edmonton: J.W. Jeffery, 1919. https://archive.org/details/albertahorsecattoounse_1/mode/2up.

Alberta Department of Agriculture. *Alberta Horse and Cattle Brands, 1919–20*. Edmonton: J.W. Jeffery, 1921. https://archive.org/details/albertahorsecattoounse_2/mode/2up .

Alberta Department of Agriculture. *Supplement to Alberta Horse and Cattle Brands, 1914*. Edmonton: J.W. Jeffery, 1915. https://archive.org/details/albertahorsecattoounse/mode/2up

Henderson, Jas. *Henderson's Rancher's Directory and Brand Book*. 1 ed. Winnipeg: W.T. Walker, 1888. https://n2t.net/ark:/69429/m0zw18k78v66; https://archive.org/details/hendersonsnorthwoounse/page/n1/mode/2up

Henderson's NorthWest Brand Book. 2 ed. Winnipeg: Henderson Directory Company, 1889. Canadiana. https://n2t.net/ark:/69429/m08p5v69cn2d

North West Brand Book. Calgary: Calgary Herald, 1900. https://n2t.net/ark:/69429/m0862b857507.

North West Brand Book: Supplement No. 1. Calgary: Calgary Herald, 1904. https://n2t.net/ark:/69429/m0862b857507.

COLOPHON

The body text is set in Martina Plantijn designed by Klim Type Foundry. Select pages showcase a font called Black Cowboy Prototype, created by Bertrand Bickersteth. It is available for public download at bertrandbickersteth.com/font and will feature in a forthcoming collection of poetry. This font was developed from the designs of Black cowboys and ranchers from the late 19th- and early 20th-century. John Ware, Alberta's famous Black cowboy, is impressed in every benign 9. David Mills, the Kainai Nation's Afro-Indigenous ancestor, sends out DMs. Benjamin Washington, the displaced Barnardo 'boy, is the *being* in BW. These letters represent the impossible return of their Black braininess, their unpredicted designs on our minds. Long-ago-orphaned to history, these foundlings of the past now make up a foundry for the future. Despite appearances, the future never forgets. History is ever present, ever remarkable.

Published by AU Press, Athabasca University
1 University Drive, Athabasca, AB T9S 3A3

https://doi.org/10.15215/aupress/ 9781771994644.01

Cover and interior design by Natalie Olsen, kisscutdesign.com
Printed and bound in Canada

CERTIFIED CANADIAN PUBLISHER

Library and Archives Canada Cataloguing in Publication
Title: Numinous animal : tracing the Afrofuturism of Black cowboys / Bertrand Bickersteth.
Names: Bickersteth, Bertrand, 1969– author.
Series: Writing in residence.
Description: Series statement: Writing in residence | Includes bibliographical references.
Identifiers: Canadiana (print) 20260166979 | Canadiana (ebook) 20260176427 | ISBN 9781771994644 (softcover) | ISBN 9781771994651 (PDF) | ISBN 9781771994668 (EPUB)
Subjects: LCSH: Black people—Prairie Provinces—History. | LCSH: Cowboys—Prairie Provinces—History. | LCSH: Cattle brands—Prairie Provinces—History. | LCSH: Afrofuturism.
Classification: LCC FC3250.B6 B53 2026 | DDC 305.896/0712—dc23

We acknowledge the financial support of the Government of Canada through the Canada Book Fund (CBF) for our publishing activities and the assistance provided by the Government of Alberta through the Alberta Media Fund.

Alberta Government Canada